MARCH 2013

To Amick——
   Lola + I ARE so
much looking FORWARD
To your "MAGIC"
At our 50th IN JUNE.
   Be well.
   All my best,

Praise for *This Is the Moment!*

"Truly magical and life-changing! A testimony that the Law of Gratitude is more powerful than the Law of Attraction, and that being there in person is the greatest gift you can bestow on those you love. A must-read for all!"

— **Denis Waitley,**
the author of *Seeds of Greatness*

"My friend Walter Green is a successful man not only personally, but professionally. In the cocktail hour of his life, he has done what few people have ever thought of doing, and that is to go back and revisit all those people in his life who assisted in propelling him forward in his journey. This is a wise, thought-provoking, and provocative endeavor, and a very interesting and inspiring read."

— **Suzanne Somers,**
TV personality and actress;
best-selling author of *Knockout*

*"There's an old adage that asks: 'Why put off until tomorrow that which you can do today?' **This Is the Moment!** is Walter Green's take on that age-old sound advice. This is not your usual 'how to' book. Rather, it's a compelling, deeply personal accounting of a life well lived and appreciated; as well as how Walter thanked those he felt were responsible for helping him live that life to the fullest, while they were still alive to hear and appreciate it. A good read and good advice. Enjoy it."*

— **Bill Bratton,**
the former chief of the LAPD and
former New York City Police Commissioner

THIS IS THE MOMENT!

Hay House Titles of Related Interest

THIS IS THE MOMENT!

How One Man's Yearlong Journey Captured the
Power of Extraordinary Gratitude

WALTER GREEN

HAY HOUSE, INC.
Carlsbad, California • New York City
London • Sydney • Johannesburg
Vancouver • Hong Kong • New Delhi

Published and distributed in the United States by: Hay House, Inc.:
www.hayhouse.com • *Published and distributed in Australia by:* Hay
House Australia Pty. Ltd.: www.hayhouse.com.au • *Published and distributed in the United Kingdom by:* Hay House UK, Ltd.: www.hayhouse
.co.uk • *Published and distributed in the Republic of South Africa by:*
Hay House SA (Pty), Ltd.: www.hayhouse.co.za • *Distributed in Canada
by:* Raincoast: www.raincoast.com • *Published in India by:* Hay House
Publishers India: www.hayhouse.co.in

Editorial supervision: Jill Kramer • *Project editor:* Shannon Littrell
Design: Jen Kennedy

Library of Congress Cataloging-in-Publication Data

Green, Walter.
  This is the moment! : how one man's yearlong journey captured the
power of extraordinary gratitude / Walter Green. -- 1st ed.
    p. cm.
  Includes bibliographical references.
  ISBN 978-1-4019-2808-7 (hardcover : alk. paper) 1. Gratitude. 2. Interpersonal relations. I. Title.
  BJ1533.G8G735 2010
  170'.44--dc22
                                                    2010016051

Hardcover ISBN: 978-1-4019-2808-7
Digital ISBN: 978-1-4019-2938-1

13 12 11 10   4 3 2 1
1st edition, October 2010

Printed in the United States of America

To my mother and father,

who gave me wings;

to my wife, Lola,

who has enriched my

flight of life beyond words;

and to our sons, Jonathan and Jason,

who filled the sky

with sunshine.

CONTENTS

FOREWORD

They say great minds think alike, and that's certainly true for me and my friend of 30 years, Walter Green. Among other things, we share a lifelong passion for celebration and appreciation.

As I was approaching my 70th birthday, I invited all of my co-authors to come to San Diego for a day-and-a-half celebration. I was thrilled that almost 50 of them accepted the invitation and came to the event, including: Don Shula, the old Miami Dolphins coach; Spencer Johnson, who wrote *The One Minute Manager* with me; Colleen Barrett, president of Southwest Airlines; Garry Ridge, president of WD-40 Company; and many of the colleagues I've written books with at the Ken Blanchard Companies. A lot of them didn't know each other, and it was a thrill to see all of these great people meeting and interacting.

Not only was it a fun way to celebrate my birthday, it was a really special event as well. We had panels and discussions on sharing the simple truths we'd learned over time about human behavior and leadership. One of the reasons I got all of these people together was because, like Walter, I'd been impacted by the book *Tuesdays with Morrie,* and how Morrie Schwartz had a kind of funeral before he died. I thought, *Wow, I'd like to have a gathering of the significant people in my life before anything happens to me.* It was an exceptional experience to celebrate and be with all those people.

I thought that my idea for getting these people together and celebrating my birthday with them was the best. Then I talked to Walter and discovered that he had topped me by quite a bit. He'd sat down and made a list of all the people who had significantly impacted his life over the years, and then he spent a year going around the country connecting with them and telling them how they'd made a difference in his life. He told them what they'd meant to him. He interviewed them and shared special moments with them. When he told me about this, I said, "What a fabulous idea for a book." Clearly, it was a case of "great minds" again, because here it is.

It's a wonderful idea to reach out and thank the people who have made a difference in our lives. Too often we think good things about others but don't take the time to let them know.

Enjoy this book of Walter's. Let it inspire you to think of the individuals who have helped you in your life. Let it move you to tell those people the positive difference they've made. And let it happen soon, because *this is the moment!*

— **Ken Blanchard,**
co-author of *The One Minute Manager®*
and *Leading at a Higher Level*

Introduction

Meaningful relationships are at the very core of my being, so when I chose to take a year to celebrate my blessings, I focused it on these life-enhancing relationships. I traveled around the country and even abroad to reconnect with 44 special people in my life. We spent time recalling the good fortune in how we met, and recollecting some of our most cherished shared experiences. Then I expressed to them, in a heartfelt way, my deep appreciation for what they'd meant to me. I knew that these men and women had been important, but while formulating these expressions of gratitude, I began to recognize that their influence had dramatically changed my life. Some were even "road-changers," especially during my formative years.

My beginnings were modest. When I was a child, my family moved every few years around New York and New Jersey as my father sought business opportunities, and we eventually ended up in Florida for his health. After college, I spent eight years in a variety of jobs, most notably in public accounting for three years and in the restaurant and hotel fields for five more years. Then I invested my limited savings in Harrison Conference Centers, a start-up company based in Glen Cove on the north shore of Long Island, New York. Harrison was also the first in the United States to develop a network of centers with its focus on small meetings for management, sales, and training.

For the next 29 years I had an extremely fulfilling and rewarding business career, most of it as Chairman, CEO, and major shareholder of what became an innovative industry leader in the executive conference center field. With nine centers in the eastern half of the United States, we had 1,400 employees hosting some 6,000 business meetings annually, which were attended by more than 150,000 conferees.

Upon selling my company about 12 years ago, my wife, Lola, and I moved to San Diego. Since then, I've achieved great personal satisfaction from focusing on those interests and activities that are meaningful and purposeful to me. And a couple of years ago, while reflecting on what I'd ideally like to have happen so that I would look back at this time and see it as an extraordinary life experience, the idea of a yearlong gratitude journey was born.

I really had no plans to write a book about all of this. Then about six months into the experience, the idea to do so kept arising. Lola and I would be dining with friends, and she'd ask me to tell them about my journey. No more than five minutes into the story, the light would go on in people's eyes when they "got" it. They'd start talking about what an expression of profound gratitude might mean in their own lives. Then, almost without exception, someone would say, "You ought to write a book." Although flattered by the compliment, I was doing this out of my own personal needs and desires, and was committed to staying totally focused on completing the journey. It was becoming clearer by the day, though, that the idea was truly resonating with those who heard about it.

The notion of writing a book was further encouraged when a couple of events convinced me that this idea had an appeal well beyond my own peer group. One was when the story moved an acquaintance who is a cigar-smoking, motorcycle-riding, card-playing "man's man." While I wouldn't have immediately identified him as someone who would have readily embraced the concept, he said that it spoke to him because of regrets he harbored about not expressing gratitude to people who were no longer here.

The second event occurred when I was in Kenya with Free The Children, the world's largest network of children helping children. There were 22 of us on the mission, including my son Jason. During lunch one day, I told my story to the organization's founder, 28-year-old Craig Kielburger, and he was so affected by it that he asked me to repeat it to everyone else after dinner that night. I did, and all in attendance gave me a standing round of applause. Granted, these were people who had flown halfway around the world to do good work and not a bunch of hard-edged, self-focused types. Nevertheless, most were considerably younger than I am and didn't have a lifetime of experience behind them. Yet they still understood that expressing gratitude to those who mattered in their lives was relevant to them.

Now recognizing the breadth of its appeal, I was coming around to thinking that this journey of mine—and all that transpired from it—perhaps *could* be a book. It came to fruition when Lola met an acquaintance named Jill Kramer for lunch one day and told her what I'd been up to for the past several months. As I joined them at the end of their get-together, I discovered that Jill also happens to be the editorial director at Hay House publishing. After I related my story in more detail, Jill expressed quite a bit of enthusiasm and stated that this could indeed be a book. She arranged for me to meet with Reid Tracy, the president of the company, the following week, and the day after that I was offered a book contract. And now you have the results in your hands.

I've chosen to break down the book into three parts:

In Part I, you'll learn much more about how and why I chose to make this voyage of gratitude. I'll explain the criteria I used to select the people on my list and tell you how I structured the journey and the meetings. You'll share in some of the nuggets of insight regarding relationships and self-discovery I unexpectedly found along the way, which may resonate with you and be important considerations in your *own* life.

One of the most surprising things for me was how my expressing gratitude to others was also beneficial to them. In this section, I also look at the downside of not doing it—namely, the pain of regret.

In Part II, you'll read my life story. You'll meet many of the people who were on my journey, and be privy to excerpts from the conversations we had (which have been edited for clarity). We generally spoke for at least an hour, and we covered a lot of ground. Therefore, I've highlighted just some of what I said, particularly that part of our conversation where I expressed my gratitude to them.

Everyone I talk about by name in this section of the book was on my list. Clearly, I couldn't include each conversation I had in full, so I've selected those that could help you identify the types of people to whom you may want to express gratitude. You'll see the variety of the men and women I selected and what part they've played in making a difference in my life.

These conversations were only ever meant to be between me and the person to whom I was expressing my appreciation, plus any loved ones we chose to share them with. But when the opportunity for me to write a book arose, everyone graciously agreed to allow me to use their names and portions of what we talked about. In addition to those on my gratitude list, there are other individuals whose stories I tell; and in some cases I've withheld or changed their names and locations to honor their privacy.

Further, I hope that reading about how I expressed my own gratitude will assist those of you who might be unsure of how to put into words what each person on *your* list means to you. I say this because drilling down this deeply is not something we do every day; nor do we have many role models or tools to help us. Most of us are only comfortable talking *about* others, whether as a eulogy or as part of everyday conversations. We're not comfortable with the idea of talking to them in a heartfelt way. So I laid some groundwork, and I hope that hearing how I approached the task will help you unlock the power of extraordinary gratitude for yourself.

Part III is all about *you*. I want to emphasize that you don't have to wait for some momentous occasion to start your own gratitude journey: it truly is never too soon. No matter what your age or stage in life, there are people—perhaps parents, grandparents, dear friends, colleagues, or teachers—who have already made a difference, and it would be wonderful to recognize them. Here you'll find the tips and tools to help you appreciate your individual road-changers or life-influencers and create your own conversations with them. I'll then try to assist you in overcoming any hesitancy you may have about undertaking your personal expressions of gratitude. Finally, I'm excited to share with you how people, some on my list and others who only heard about it, have already started paying it forward in unexpected ways.

❦ ❦ ❦

I do not come to this subject as a scholar or a researcher in the field of gratitude. However, I did walk this walk and will be sharing a real experience with you. I wrote this book for *you*. If, as a result of reading it, you take action, I believe you'll find this path to be extraordinarily gratifying. Additionally, knowing that you have done so will be very gratifying for *me*.

❦ ❦ ❦ ❦

PART I

MY JOURNEY

CHAPTER ONE

An Idea Whose Time Has Come

"At times our own light goes out and is rekindled by a spark from another person. Each of us has cause to think with deep gratitude of those who have lighted the flame within us."

— ALBERT SCHWEITZER

Looking back on my life, I recognize that it's been filled with many gratifying high points. This is especially so considering my difficult early start. Upon hearing my story in subsequent chapters, you might be tempted to see it as a typical rags-to-riches tale about a self-made man. But what I've come to learn as a result of this past year is that it's anything but that.

Once I became really conscious, I realized that although I've worked hard and been lucky, I'm the furthest thing from self-made. On the contrary, I've been "made" to a large extent by the quality of some of the people I've known and the profound influence they've had on my life. This process made me wonder whether I could have achieved what I did without them: The conclusion I came to is that I couldn't. I'm not being modest; I'm calling it like it is, and it's been a very humbling experience.

It wasn't just humbling but also very satisfying to know that I had the good fortune to have these individuals play the role they did in my life. Candidly, though, I didn't always think about all the ways they had impacted me. It was not a conscious part of my remembrance of them.

In his book *Thanks!: How Practicing Gratitude Can Make You Happier,* Robert Emmons, Ph.D., writes: "We can be proud of our accomplishments yet simultaneously realize they would have been impossible without help from others. This realization is the soil that permits gratitude to germinate."

My plan, then, was to revisit those influential men and women and express, in an uncommon way, my profound appreciation to them. By "uncommon," I mean going beyond the customary "Thank you" that we routinely utter after an act of kindness, a favor, or a nice dinner spent together; or what I call "episodic" gratitude. It's entirely different to look back on our lives and articulate how aware we are of the way someone has impacted it and let him or her know. I refer to this as "systemic" gratitude.

You might think of this as the difference between the Oscars and the Kennedy Center Honors. At the former, winners are singled out for excellence in a specific piece of work; that is, an Academy Award represents a onetime expression of appreciation. At the latter, honorees are celebrated by a succession of their peers who have been influenced, inspired, motivated, enriched, and even sent down a new path by these artists or their work. The Kennedy Center Honors ceremony often features moving tributes by colleagues who make it very clear how the honorees' lifetime contribution to the arts has mattered to them personally.

Also, uncommon and explicit expressions of gratitude are something quite distinct from what I call "living tributes" and eulogies.

Living tributes tend to be situational and specific. We make them at events such as weddings, retirements, or award ceremonies; or after some heroic deed has been performed. Living tributes are often public and quite short, and they're usually inadequate when it comes to conveying deep appreciation for those contributions that have made a long-term difference in our lives.

When it comes to eulogies, these occasions do serve the purpose of acknowledging individuals in the company of others. When we speak so eloquently about those who have died, we often feel that we're speaking to them; saying what we always wanted to say and having them actually listen. But since we're only speaking about them, this missed opportunity can cause us pain and regret. Additionally, only a small number of family members and friends get the honor of speaking, and more than 95 percent of people who knew the deceased don't have an opportunity to say anything. Plus, most eulogies are short, maybe five minutes at most.

Gratitude Is More Than Attitude

I've given a lot of thought to the subject of gratitude before, during, and after my yearlong journey. For a long time, I've regularly expressed appreciation for how our lives are made easy by everyday conveniences. Each morning, for instance, I marvel that I can turn a piece of metal in the shower and out comes clean water; and by adjusting that lever, I can make the water warmer or cooler! That's pretty amazing when you think about it, and what a great way to become awake and aware every day. When I got down to writing this book, I was grateful that I live in a time when I could do it on a computer and not have to labor with a pen and paper.

More important, I'm grateful to just be alive. My first thought every morning when I open my eyes is, *Thank You, God, for another day; another day to do good things*. My father died when he was 53, and I've always thought that living beyond that age would be an extraordinary achievement. Now that I have, I'm finding every additional day a real gift. Right behind that is my level of fitness, which allows me to take pleasure in those activities I enjoy. I'm also so thankful for the love I have for my wife, Lola, and our sons. In fact, my entire extended family and my community of friends are central to my being, and I've always worked hard at nurturing and maintaining those relationships.

By investing decades in a demanding job and encountering some good fortune and good people along the way, I now have the resources to enjoy a comfortable lifestyle that I fully appreciate. But more than that, after years of focusing thoughtfully on my life, I am very clear about what speaks to me, and am profoundly grateful for the fact that I'm able to spend most of my time on matters that are really important to me. My activities are very much in alignment with my life's purpose. What more could I ask for.

The idea of "counting your blessings" is a cornerstone of many faiths. It's also been covered in books and the media and has even been the subject of academic research. We're urged to develop an "attitude of gratitude" and keep note of it in our journals. I refer to these types of practices as internally directed gratitude: we're talking to ourselves. Using an anatomical metaphor, it's like a muscle that needs to be exercised in order for us to get full benefits.

Externally focused gratitude—expressed directly to others—is another muscle that needs to be exercised as well. One of the many lessons I learned is that the more you exercise that external gratitude muscle by telling others how you feel about them, the more benefits you *and* they get.

Yet although we often express appreciation for certain people in our journals, or even speak to others about them, we don't tend to express it to the person in question. It's like the father who tells his buddies how wonderful his son is, but never shares this directly with the young man. So everybody else knows how proud the father feels, but the son has little idea and might even have a totally erroneous view of his father's opinion of him. In too many cases, these stories are shared with the son by others only after the father has died.

I believe that situations like this are not only unfortunate, but they're missed opportunities, too. I hope that as you read on, you'll awaken to your own opportunities and not let them pass by.

◎ ◎ ◎

Even though I'd always placed a high value on my own relationships, amazingly, I'd never specifically articulated to these individuals what each of them meant to me. These conversations I now planned were a chance for me to communicate explicit and genuine expressions of appreciation to those who have enriched my life in so many ways. This truly was going to be an out-of-the-ordinary experience.

Deep and heartfelt conversation has always been an essential element of my interactions with people.

In other words, while we might enjoy a round of golf or traveling together, the time we spent was as much about the high-quality conversations after the game or during the trip. Nevertheless, there were still important things left unsaid.

During the planning stages of my gratitude journey, I began to affectionately refer to this project as my "victory lap" because it had all the connotations of celebration and appreciation. I was reminded of basketball icon Michael Jordan, who paid a visit to all the arenas he'd played in during his career as a gesture to thank his fans upon his retirement. Not that I'm in any way retiring from life (I feel as good today as I ever have and am probably in better shape than I have been in years), nor do I consider the people on my victory lap to be "fans." What our journeys have in common, though, is the profound appreciation we share for those who supported our life to date and without whom we couldn't have done what we did.

My own journey would actually include several trips, in which I'd deliver my gratitude while I still had the energy and before it was too late and the opportunity was lost. I didn't want to wait until any of our lives were compromised by ill health or imminent death. So I figured that I should tell these people how much they mattered to me long—hopefully, very long—before that happened and I was left with regrets.

The Idea Is Born

Like all viable ideas, the recipe for this one had many ingredients. The first ones I can identify are my parents' health crises. My mother had two bouts with breast cancer, the first when I was just 9; and my father had a heart attack when I was 11 that he survived, but subsequently had a fatal one when I was 17. These were lessons that awakened me to how short and precious life can be. What a bittersweet gift.

As an adult, I became fascinated with learning about life from studying death, and I'm still drawn to books on these subjects. Among those that got me thinking about my gratitude journey are: Mitch Albom's *Tuesdays with Morrie,* which I read several years ago; and, more recently, Randy Pausch's *The Last Lecture* and Eugene O'Kelly's *Chasing Daylight.*

An imperative to express unsaid thoughts and feelings before time ran out was a common thread in all three books. In the case of *Tuesdays with Morrie,* the title character was aged and in poor health; in the other two, the authors were far younger but had received diagnoses that left them facing impending death. These books drove home the point that when time gets short, conversations become real, and messages that we want to leave to those we care about—be they our spouse, children, family, friends, or colleagues—take on critical importance. So it occurred to me that if these conversations are so crucial at the end, why not have them earlier? Why not have them *now?* And that was the idea that gave birth to the title of my book: *This Is the Moment!*

Another thing that affected me related to this subject was the sudden death of NBC political commentator Tim Russert. Only 58 years old and clearly respected in his profession, he received tributes from presidents and politicians, colleagues and comedians, and even rock stars. His death was so fast and unexpected that those who were greatly indebted to him and loved him for all he'd done were cheated out of being able to tell him what he'd meant to them. What a shame that the impact of the extraordinary tributes at his funeral was offset by the awareness that he would never hear the difference he'd made in so many people's lives.

I'm not suggesting that Tim Russert had such a powerful ego that he needed to hear all of these tributes, but I do believe that most of us receive value from acknowledgment by others. In fact, I've long been conscious of the power of gratitude. I've also had a commitment to leading a meaningful life and maintained an appreciation of the central role that relationships have played in creating that meaning.

Foreshadowing this current journey, some years ago on my birthday I made a short list of close friends whom I felt had deeply influenced me. I invited them to a weekend event and publicly thanked them for adding richness to all areas of my life: intellectual, emotional, physical, and financial. Another time, I kept a log for three months of my acts of kindness and began to pay attention to their impact.

Sadly, however, the two people who brought me into this world have passed away, and I missed my opportunity to be explicit with either of them about what they had meant to me. I was greatly affected by this and wanted to be sure that there would be no further regrets in this regard.

My hope was that by the end of my yearlong journey, the people who were so special to me would be aware of why I loved them and why I so appreciated them. If I were to pass away unexpectedly after the last conversation, no one would have to worry about what I would have said to or about them, or what they would have said to or about me.

The Plan Takes Shape

It was an ambitious plan, and implementing it required my wife's blessing and support. When I first brought up the idea, Lola was truly concerned about how I was going to fit all these visits into my whirlwind life of mentoring, coaching, and philanthropic endeavors; splitting time between two homes; a disciplined exercise program; and extensive travel. It wasn't until I assured her that I'd do it over the course of a year that she enthusiastically championed the cause and told me that she'd do whatever it took to help me make it work.

A lot of thought went into the planning of my year. First, I had to make a list of the individuals I wanted to visit. There have been many men and women who have been important in my life and who mattered, but for this purpose, I was specifically thinking about the "life-changers" who'd had an effect on me in meaningful ways.

I looked back over the years and realized that they came from all walks of life: business associates; medical, health, and financial advisors; mentees; colleagues in the nonprofit world; members of organizations I belonged to; and of course, dear friends and family members. These were the people who have been with me through tough times; those who have steered me on a different course; and the professionals who have given me peace of mind in different areas of my life.

When I focused on it, there turned out to be 44 names on my list, which surprised even me (but I've probably been around longer than many of you!). They came from vastly diverse backgrounds. Some had very simple lifestyles, two were billionaires, and there was everything in between. They ranged in age from 28 to 87. There were more men than women. While some were members of my family, most were not.

Based on responses from those I've talked to about my journey, I know you might also be thinking, *I don't have 44 people; nothing close.* That's okay. Even if just one person immediately comes to mind, you'll find value in reading further. Expressing profound gratitude to that one human being will likely enrich your life and the lives of others as well. I promise that by the end of this book, you'll be giving thought to more people.

Next, I had to determine what I was going to say to these 44 individuals. I was very clear about the outcomes I intended for these conversations and decided that in order to achieve them, I wanted to touch four bases:

First, we'd start out by reflecting on when we'd first met. I've known the participants on my journey an average of just over a quarter of a century, which is particularly remarkable in light of the fact that the only person on my list who knew me before the age of 17 was my older brother, Ray. Some of these relationships went back 40 years, almost all were a decade or more long, and nobody went back less than 5 years. I couldn't actually remember how I'd met some of my old friends, but I knew that one or the other of us would recall the details and we'd piece it together. I figured that beginning in this way would provide an easy entrée into the conversation.

Second, I wanted to evoke some of the memorable life experiences and activities that we'd shared. As we began to reminisce, I'd allow the conversation to go wherever it went. It was not my intention to impose a rigid structure. I anticipated that these trips down memory lane would be a real pleasure. It was also a way of "setting the table" for the next part of our conversation.

Third, this was what the meeting was really all about: my opportunity to say, "You've had a great effect on me, and I want to be abundantly clear with you about how you've influenced my life, and to explicitly express my gratitude to you for what you've meant to me." While that was the crux of the conversation, every expression of appreciation was to be crafted specifically for each individual. Going through this process for all 44 people on my list required me to be very conscious and deliberate. When I heard the concept that gratitude is like turning on a flashlight in a dark room—everything was in there already, it just had to be illuminated—I could truly relate to that.

Fourth, for my self-enlightenment, I'd give each person a minute or two to present his or her perceptions of me. Put together, their perspectives would form a composite view of me that clearly would be more accurate than a self-portrait. I envisioned it as everyone placing a piece in a mosaic that made up the complete picture of who I am. If they wanted to share any feelings about me, that would be special as well.

   ℞ ℞ ℞

I invited these people, either in person or by way of a phone call, to join me on this journey. They were scattered around the country, and in some instances we'd gotten together infrequently over the years, although that didn't influence how close I felt to them. Taking the time to travel wherever they were to meet them clearly established that this visit was very important to me.

After someone heard what I wanted to do, it was quite common for the person to ask, "Are you okay?" Even after I responded that I was, he or she would ask, "Are you sure?" My friends' reference point, as it is for our society in general, is that conversations like these are usually initiated when someone is close to death. I had to reassure them this was not the case with me.

As part of the preparation for our meetings, I sent each person an e-mail describing the four bases I wanted to cover. From my years working in the conference business, I know that people always want to be prepared for what they're going to be talking about at meetings. I knew that my friends were a little surprised by my call, and I felt that I needed to send them something in writing so they'd have a better idea of what was going to happen, and to give them time to think about our conversation in advance of the day.

When it came time to set up the meetings, I tried to choose a quiet, private location for them. Some took place in the person's own home, others in hotel rooms or private offices including my own, and some in a quiet corner of a club one or the other of us belonged to. I wanted the day to include other informal time together after each of these focused dialogues.

So if we'd played golf in the past, that could follow our talk. At a minimum, we'd have lunch or dinner.

Prior to the meetings, my preparations included making notes of my recollections of when we met and some of the highlights of our relationship over the years. But most important, I made a bullet-pointed list of answers to this question: "What difference did this person make in my life?" I went through this process with all of the people on my list, and I did refer to the notes during the meetings. It was not intrusive in the least and served me well in making sure that I didn't forget anything I wanted to say, which is easy to do when you get caught up in reminiscing and enjoying the moment. (Some people had done their own preparation as well. For example, one guy actually brought his laptop with his preparatory notes on it.)

I didn't want to take notes during these interactions so that I could stay fully engaged and savor every moment. A friend suggested that I make an audio recording of each conversation. I hadn't thought about doing so, but once it was mentioned, I realized what a great idea it was. These were going to be emotionally rich conversations, and there was no way that I'd be able to absorb and remember all of the substance and subtlety contained in them.

In advance of each conversation, I did, of course, confirm that the person would be okay with my recording him or her. There was some hesitancy from only one individual when I first raised the subject of an audio recording, but in the end he was fine with it. I bought an inconspicuous 1" x 3" digital recorder for the purpose.

Finally, I decided to bring my camera and have a photograph taken with each person as a pictorial reminder of our special time together.

The First Step

My friends were scattered around the country, so in the interests of efficiency and economy, I grouped them together. For example, for my first trip I flew to the Southeast to sit down individually with six long-time friends who lived in Georgia, Florida, and North Carolina.

I had no idea what this experience was going to be like. But if I needed any confirmation that I was on the right course, those initial meetings served that purpose. Having such focused conversations was like seeing my old friends in high definition. I was gratified to find that they enjoyed the process, and I suspect that our conversations may have meant as much to them as they did to me. I'd go so far as to say that from the standpoints of friendship, life enrichment, and self-enlightenment, they were the most remarkable eight days of my life up to that date. And I still had 38 more people to go! I could not wait to continue on my adventure. Over the next 11 months, I traveled throughout the United States, as well as Mexico and Kenya, to do just that.

❦ ❦ ❦

I cannot fully put into words how incredible this journey turned out to be for me. I did anticipate that a certain level of satisfaction would be achieved when I embarked upon it, but I could never have known the full extent of what it would mean in my life. Nor could I have foreseen the profound and unexpected results, which were above and beyond anything I could have ever imagined.

❦ ❦ ❦ ❦

CHAPTER TWO

What Did I Really Get from This?

*"Let us be grateful to people who make us happy;
they are the charming gardeners who
make our souls blossom."*

— Marcel Proust

As it turned out, the conversations I'd planned exceeded all of my expectations. It was enlightening to reflect on how I'd met these special people, for it served as a reminder of the value of intentionality. It also underscored the serendipitous way important relationships are born, along with the diversified nature of these connections.

Our walks down memory lane were joyful, reinforcing the fabric of these special, long-term relationships. What a moving experience it was to review the highlights—both successes and challenges—over the life of these interactions. The joyful experiences far outweighed the more difficult ones, but it was being there and supporting each other during the tough times that fostered our deep and lasting bonds. Every person on my list and I had encountered some serious life issues together. I'm convinced that without these challenges, life would have been far easier, but the relationships would have been far less significant and may not have even stood the test of time.

Making the time to see each of "my 44" personally gave me the additional thrill of physically being with them. When it came to four people whom I hadn't seen in a decade and had only spoken to a couple times over that period, I loved finding out that in no way had that absence of contact diminished the power and richness of the experience.

I happen to be a big hugger, and those embraces were memorable moments for me. I also loved that time after the conversations when we went for a walk, shared a meal, or engaged in some other activity together. This built on the emotional impact of the gratitude conversation and allowed us to just celebrate the moment and all that we meant to each other. We were also able to get current on each other's lives. Of course I hope to see most of these people again, but there's always the chance I might not get to due to unforeseen developments. No matter what happens, no one can take the memory of our special day from either of us.

These were all outcomes that I might have expected at the beginning of this journey. But along the way I also stumbled across pure gold, which yielded more unexpected treasures than I could have ever anticipated.

One evening after I'd completed my yearlong journey of gratitude, I told my story at a social event. As Lola and I were leaving, a friend stopped me and said that he had one more question. "What did *you* get from all this?" he asked. "What was it really like for you?" It was almost as if he were asking me to reveal a secret, and it prompted me to drill a little deeper for a response.

The very first thing that occurred to me in answer to his question was: *peace of mind.* I didn't realize I was getting it at the time I was having my conversations or even after I'd finished them. I only got in touch with how peaceful I'd become sometime later when I was faced with a crisis.

A Tale of Two Cruises

After finishing my 44th conversation and before starting work on this book, Lola and I decided to go on a Caribbean cruise. Halfway into the trip, we were at a fairly major port when I felt chest pains and had to see the ship's doctor. He discovered that I had an abnormal EKG, and my blood pressure was 50 percent higher than it usually was. Given my father's early death from a heart attack, I was afraid that I might be following in his footsteps.

Since the next port was a remote island with no hospital or airport, I had to make an immediate decision about what to do. I chose to leave the ship and fly home so that I could consult my own doctors. As it turned out, it was a muscular problem in the chest area, and I'm fine.

This was not the first time I'd had to cut a cruise short. Just two years earlier, Lola and I had embarked upon one in the Mediterranean with a group of about 100 people, all of us members of clubs from our community. A few days into the cruise, I began experiencing what was initially diagnosed as indigestion but which turned out to be a life-threatening strangulated hernia. I had to leave the ship immediately, and I found myself on the island of Corsica, where I knew no one and had no resources. Frankly, I was panicked on top of being seriously ill.

By good fortune, my friend Jeff Stiefler happened to be on the cruise, too. Without even being asked, he left his wife aboard and got off the ship with Lola and me. With calmness and good humor, he helped us cope with all that had to be done, and he stayed with us to see that my operation had gone successfully before flying to catch up with his wife at a later port of call. I'm not sure how I would have gotten through that experience without this amazing act of friendship.

I was overwhelmed by the fear of losing my life, but I had another source of anxiety as well. I knew in my heart and soul that I hadn't said everything I really wanted to say to those who have mattered in my life.

That experience and my subsequent one in the Caribbean were like before-and-after emotional x-rays. I had two similar circumstances with two very different reactions. On the cruise we took after my year of gratitude, I was no longer overwhelmed by those emotions when faced with a life-or-death situation. I felt peaceful knowing that those significant people unequivocally knew how important they were in my life. Plus, there was an audio recording of our conversation that they could listen to if something happened to me. In turn, I knew how everyone felt about me, and it was as if I'd already been to my own funeral and heard the eulogies.

This sense of completeness was never a part of my intentions for my gratitude journey, but it turned out to be a wonderful by-product of it. If that peace of mind had been the only outcome, then my journey was worth taking. I came to this epiphany in that moment when I thought my life might possibly end prematurely.

It's noteworthy that there are many books published and countless experts in the media to advise you on the mechanics of how to get your financial house in order. You get ample advice on how you need to have a file containing all of your bank-account numbers, your insurance policies, the contacts for your advisors, and so forth, and to make sure your spouse knows how to find it. I've always been meticulous about these things, and it's been reassuring to know that my wife is aware of where everything is and whom to speak to if something should happen to me. It never occurred to me to think about getting my *emotional* house in order. Certainly, I didn't know how doing so could affect the quality of my life.

And that was not the only unexpected outcome from my gratitude journey.

A Picture Tells a Thousand Words

My journey was primarily an experience focused on the 44 individuals I'd put on my list. So although the "fourth base" of my conversations was to ask the other person for a brief sentence about me for my mosaic, it wasn't initially a particularly significant component of the process.

I soon realized that I was talking to people who have known me collectively for more than a thousand years! And that's why I ultimately took advantage of the fact that I'll never again be able to access that many human beings who know me so well. As a person who likes to exploit opportunities, I began to formulate some questions in my mind, such as: *What have I learned over the years?* And most important: *How have I touched these men and women?*

My long-term friends provided a mirror that helped me see who I was when I was a young adult and how I had formed as a person. Listening to the audio recordings later was like hearing an oral history of the highlights of my life so far. Their pieces of input allowed me a unique opportunity to answer the question: *Who am I?* What an empowering gift! I never set out with an agenda of learning about myself; doing so was parenthetical and incidental, but not inconsequential.

Not only that, it started me thinking about my personal legacy. We all have a perception of ourselves, and everything we do is consistent with that vision—our integrity, our energy, our performance, our giving to others. This leads us to keep an internal scorecard and wonder how we're doing. *Am I doing the right things? Am I doing enough?* But our scorecard gets buried with us. When we're gone, only the perceptions others have of us live on. So hearing how others saw me allowed me to know how I would be remembered.

Yet this was far more than an exercise in self-absorption. Learning about myself was a way to increase my contribution to others going forward. The same themes and common threads came up over and over when my 44 talked about what they'd gotten from the relationship and how they perceived me. I also learned that our impact on people is not about what it costs us in time and effort and thought, but is really about the experience from their point of view.

I'll never forget the words shared by my son Jonathan during our poignant conversation. He said that we'd been watching the "same movie" for years but had never talked about it at this deep a level. We were not only celebrating our similarities, we were expressing gratitude for what we'd learned from our differences as well. Jonathan further shared that the joyfulness of our happy times together was that much more important and special because, he said, I was still his go-to guy after all these years.

@ @ @

We all do some things in life automatically, and that doesn't diminish the value of them. As my friend Stephen Kaufman, a senior lecturer at Harvard Business School (and one of my 44), told me, "Many times we fail to realize that simple, off-the-cuff comments or reactions that don't really register with us can touch important nerves or strike chords in others. My students and former colleagues often drop me notes referring to something I did or said five or ten years ago as having had a deep impact on them, yet at the time they just seemed to me like ordinary conversations with no particular import."

I had the pleasure of sharing one of my conversations with Joel Richey, a talented and caring physical therapist, who for the past 15 years has worked with me to prevent the excruciating back spasms I used to regularly experience. During my now-infrequent bouts of physical discomfort, he reduces the pain level 50 percent and cuts the number of days' duration by half. He's given me one of life's greatest gifts: the pleasure of almost pain-free living.

In the process of expressing my gratitude to Joel, he expressed his thankfulness for the contributions

I'd made to him by asking questions about key issues in his life and sharing my own experiences. This had particular meaning to me. I only see Joel when I go for treatment, and during that time I'm mostly lying on my back. To be reminded of the variety of ways in which we impact people—no matter what our condition or position or locale—left an indelible impression on me.

Being made aware of the value to others of what we do and say made me vividly conscious of how I might be more helpful in the future as well. I could look at something specific and recognize how it made a difference. I had a remarkable opportunity to see how doing more of it would be of even greater value to those I care about.

Also, the common threads that permeated these significant life relationships served as a "criteria sieve" in deciding which new relationships to nurture going forward in life. I realized that my criteria were loyalty, trust, integrity, shared values, and the capacity for deep conversations and laughter. So while it might seem at first glance that this was an exercise in looking back, it bore remarkable implications for the future.

The Happiness Factor

On my journey, I found that expressing gratitude was certainly pleasurable in the moment, but it elevated my general sense of happiness, too. The scientific community, which has studied this very topic, backs up what I've experienced. Findings have shown that those who are acknowledged and appreciated feel valued, but those bestowing the praise reap tremendous benefits as well, which is something to which I can now testify.

The investigators of the Research Project on Gratitude and Thankfulness at UC Davis have studied gratitude's effect on our general well-being. They discovered that people who have what they call a "grateful disposition" experience high levels of life satisfaction, vitality, and optimism; along with lower levels of depression and stress. Author Robert Emmons, who was one of the researchers, characterizes gratitude as the forgotten factor in happiness research.

Others also believe that gratitude is a major component in happiness. In her book, *The How of Happiness,* author Sonja Lyubomirsky cites eight ways in which gratitude boosts happiness, including that it can "help build social bonds, strengthening existing relationships and nurturing new ones."

Dr. Martin Seligman, who promotes the concept of positive psychology, has said that "expressing gratitude has surprisingly wide-ranging benefits to both the recipient and the person conveying appreciation." And that was one of the monumental revelations I got from this process: that my recipients were being gifted with some of the same benefits that I was.

❦ ❦ ❦

Without a doubt, these conversations were defining moments in my long-term friendships. My expressions of profound gratitude have added a new level of meaning to these relationships that served as a platform for even more respect, appreciation, and love in the future.

CHAPTER THREE

WHAT OTHERS GOT FROM THIS

*"How each friend represents a world in us,
a world possibly not born
until they arrive . . ."*

— ANÄIS NIN

I want to be very clear and candid about the fact that when I started out on this journey, it was all about *me!* Telling people what they meant to me was my gift to myself. Even though the words and the expressions of gratitude were directed at them, it was my way to make sure that they knew how I felt about them. There was no element of "payback" involved. It was about the pleasure I got from giving.

Almost everyone loves to give gifts, and personal presents always garner the most appreciation in return. What could be more personal than an expression of gratitude? Each expression I made was like an individual gift that I'd wrapped in my preparatory thoughts, and it was pure joy to for me to offer it to those on my list.

Then something interesting happened. In the process of serving myself and feeling good about what I was doing, I began to realize that this victory lap of mine was turning out to be pleasurable and meaningful for my life-changers, too. As my friend John Galston told me, "Those of us who were tapped for participation in your victory lap genuinely received as much as we hope *you* did from the experience."

I'd go further and say that this was a powerful experience for many of these individuals. Over and over I heard back that people were happy, felt honored and special, and were moved to be a recipient of this gift.

Here are excerpts from some of the other responses I got:

- "Your journey was all about the human connection. I feel very fortunate to have heard what I did at this stage of my life. It was profound, and further enriched our relationship." — **Jonathan Green**

- "You shined your light on me, and I felt a sense of value that my life meant something more than I thought it did." — **Andrew Zenoff**

- "I was completely and totally honored to have been included in such an awe-inspiring process and event. I feel strongly that we should try to communicate how we feel to our loved ones. You have taken that so many steps further and created a blueprint for others to follow." — **Christy Barwick**

- "I was profoundly privileged to be part of your journey. It rekindled the 40-plus years our relationship has endured, and the pleasure and satisfaction associated with it." — **Jerry DeSimone**

It became very clear to me that the gift of gratitude for someone deepens the relationship with him or her.

I also began to recognize that another aspect of this project was that it gave others an opportunity to reciprocate. By my setting up the conversation, they came to realize that they could express some of their thoughts about *me,* which they might never have done otherwise.

Chuck Heilbrunn, my friend and physician, said how happy he was that he'd had the chance to tell me what I meant to him, and our conversation "set the table" and allowed that to happen.

I heard something similar from others, as well:

- "You thought *you* were the one expressing gratitude. Not so fast! The beauty of the road you paved was that it was a two-way street. Thanks for the opportunity to allow 44 individuals to express their gratitude to you." — **Tommy Schulhof**

- "I think it's a gift to give others the opportunity to talk about what you've meant to them. I very much appreciate that you allowed me to do this with you." — **Vicki Peterson**

- "It was revealing to me to dig deep to try to articulate in turn what I had learned from you over the years, the impact that you've had on me, and the value of our friendship to me. Writing this made me realize how bad I would have felt had I not expressed my own gratitude to you." — **Andy Potash**

I definitely got the sense that my friends appreciated the opportunity to share some thoughts about me, and they were glad that they wouldn't have to live with regrets should anything happen to me. But there was more. The power of self-recognition that they got from my acknowledging who they were was another one of the unexpected gifts they received from the experience.

It's clear to me that in highlighting people's contribution to *my* life, they could more fully appreciate the impact they had on others. A few of them said that they never realized what they were doing in terms of friendships. I bet they began to think, *If I did this to help Walter and it meant so much to him, I can do it more often in the future for others.*

In addition to these responses, I also heard reports of how many of my 44 were planning to give this gift of gratitude to others in their own lives in the future, or were actually doing so already. You'll read some of those remarkable stories later.

Memories Are Made of This

After seeing how much our encounters meant to one another, I decided it would be fitting to give each person a vivid reminder so that he or she could be sure of just how much I appreciated his or her participation in my victory lap. I wanted it to be something permanent that the individual could save and savor and share with loved ones if he or she so chose. So I created an individual memento of our time together. This was all about my 44 and quite separate from my original journey and intentions, and it was something I gave a lot of thought to.

First, I had each of the conversations I'd recorded made into a CD. I'd originally recorded them because I knew that our dialogue would be rich and I'd never be able to remember everything the person talked about.

Now I realized that he or she probably hadn't retained any more of what we'd talked about than I had. Since these conversations were so important, I wanted my friend to have what I'd secured for myself: the ability to relive them. And it seems like that was the case.

"I've listened to the CD you sent quite a few times," said Chuck Heilbrunn. "Like the afternoon we spent talking together, it evokes some very deep feelings and memories. That CD is very important to me, and I enjoy it immensely."

Another component of each memento was a copy of the photograph I'd taken of the two of us at our meeting. Every time I look at these pictures, they are instant reminders of the wonderful times I spent with my treasured friends. So I framed each photo along with an individual handwritten note from me, which summarized my appreciation of them.

I have to mention the unexpected pleasure that resulted from the excitement generated by those who helped me assemble these keepsakes, including: Joe Goodwin, who created the CDs in his San Diego sound studio; Cary Morgan, who produced the individual photographs and the CD jacket covers; and Adrian Fortmann, who designed and made the wonderful frames. They couldn't have been more engaged and enthused about the project, and did everything possible to make their contribution special. It was as if they were on the journey with me, and it was yet another indication that this concept of gratitude was embracing all those within its reach.

I gift wrapped each framed memento and CD, and enclosed my two-page letter that described what this yearlong journey had meant to me. Every one of my 44 friends received his or her package a day or two before the end of this remarkable year.

Perhaps one of the most surprising and satisfying responses to the memento was from one of the few who initially wasn't sold on the idea of having a gratitude conversation with me.

Edgar Cullman was very forthright about the fact that when I first approached him about this, he was not interested in participating; such a concept was just not for him. But he reconsidered after talking to a mutual friend, who convinced Edgar to go ahead with it because of how much it meant to me. "After all," he said, "what's friendship about if not to understand what's important to the other person?"

I appreciated Edgar's candor and thought it was a testament to the depth of our relationship. So it was gratifying to get this response from him regarding my memento: "Because the moment was captured, I plan to hang it in a special place in my home."

Were these gifts worth all the trouble I went through? The eloquent Lisa Ligouri, one of my mentees, said it all: "Each part of it is a treasure! Every detail holds special meaning. Your letter is a beautiful summary of what the victory lap was and what it meant to be a part of it. The CD is a gift of encouragement and a special memory that will endure, speaking to me throughout my lifetime. The photo is dear to my heart. The plaque has just become the focal point of my special wall, where I put my most cherished and sentimental possessions from those people closest to me."

More evidence of the value of the gifts in cementing the experience as momentous came in some of the 30-plus e-mails I received in response to it. Here are some of the wonderful words contained therein:

- "The framed picture, the audio disc, and the wonderful handwritten note that I received from you as a wonderful memento put the experience over the top. This gesture cemented our relationship even more, if possible." — **Denny Davis**

- "The gesture of sending a CD of our conversation and the plaque was a lovely thing to do, adding to the sense that this had been an important experience for us both." — **Ellen Herrenkohl**

- "I received the beautiful package, which I shared with my family. I was very touched, Walter, that you went the extra mile to make this more meaningful. I'll cherish this memento forever." — **Alan Gleicher**

- "I've read and reread your letter and continue to marvel at the depth and sincerity of your words. They certainly capture the essence of our relationship, and for that I will be forever grateful." — **Michael Mack**

I wanted to do something different and special for Lola and our two sons, so I compiled all of the 44 conversations and downloaded them onto an iPod for each of them. Listening to this unique playlist would enable them to have that complete mosaic that everyone had contributed to, which also reflected the essence of my legacy.

Handing all of these packages off to the shipper officially brought the journey to an end (or so I thought at the time!) and gave me a great sense of accomplishment. Putting the mementos together was a long and laborious job. I realize it was also an extravagant one, but I chose to devote my time and resources to it because these relationships were that important to me.

Not everyone needs to do all of this, any more than everyone will have 44 people on his or her list. Often we can make a difference to others and vice versa with very little expenditure of time, effort, or money. The purpose and the benefits are far more crucial than the form.

Finally, I want to point out that my gift had a "head fake" in it, as Randy Pausch said in his book

The Last Lecture. His head fake was that the intent of his lecture to his students was really to create a video for his own kids. Mine was that I gave out these CDs to those on my list as a reminder of our conversations, but now they also had a keepsake for their loved ones with someone who held them dear and who expressed his heartfelt appreciation and gratitude.

I told these men and women that I wanted them to have a CD as a reminder of our time together, but I also really wanted their families to have it, knowing that it was unlikely that any of my life-changers would ever leave the sound of his or her voice on a recording for family members.

❧ ❧ ❧

I'm not just exhilarated by the pleasure my 44 and I received from expressing our gratitude to one another; the thought of not doing so is distressing. I often think, *Is there anybody else I'd regret that I didn't have a conversation with?* Having now gone on this journey, I realize how important it is and how deep our regrets can be when we don't tell others what is in our hearts.

CHAPTER FOUR

THE PAIN OF REGRET

*"The bitterest tears shed over graves
are for words left unsaid and
deeds left undone."*

— HARRIET BEECHER STOWE

Given the benefits of expressing gratitude to others, both for ourselves and the recipients, why don't we "just do it"? Well, there are strong cultural and traditional customs holding some of us back. One recent study at George Mason University in Virginia, for instance, has shown that men (particularly older men) are less likely than women to express gratitude. The researchers suggest that this is because men are socialized as children to control and conceal their softer emotions.

One of my 44, Robert Kushell, communicated this point well. "We all bear the scars of how we were raised and how society viewed respective gender roles during our growing-up years," he told me. "Men did not use the word *love* in relationship to other males. My father could never say that to me because his father never said it to him."

Over the several decades that I've been close to Bob and his family, he's been a model of support, affection, and respect for his sons. He vividly demonstrates how we have the power to change these patterns. Bob is being modest when he notes, "As a parent, I tried to change some of the ways I expressed and showed my feelings to my boys, but even then I was not as open as people are today."

In *Wisdom of Our Fathers*, Tim Russert talked about how affected his father, "Big Russ," was by the tribute to him in Tim's book *Big Russ & Me*. Tim related that a few months after the book came out, he was getting ready to leave for the airport after a family Thanksgiving holiday when his father came over to him to say good-bye. Tim wrote: "For as long as I can remember, Dad and I had always parted with a handshake and a half hug. But this time he gave me a huge bear hug and said softly, 'I love you'—something I had never heard him say before. I was fifty-four years old and all I could think was, *Boy, I wish I had written this book thirty years earlier!*"

Hopefully, when fathers or mothers read stories like this, they might consider becoming even more expressive, and without their sons or daughters having to write a book!

Although many people today really are more comfortable expressing their feelings, I think it's probably now a matter of priorities. Expressing gratitude to others is just not perceived as being that important. We're all so busy that we don't step back and reflect on what could, and likely will, be a significant missed opportunity.

After my conversation with my nephew, Eric Herrenkohl, he said, "I've been so busy recently that I've accepted I can never get it all done. So at the beginning of almost every day, I ask myself: *What's the most important thing I can do next?* If I don't know, I review my to-do list and prioritize it in light of what I want to accomplish. I say this because when I review a to-do list that has *Meet with Mom and Dad and tell them why they've been so important to me* on it, it's impossible to find an item that's more of a priority. At that point, I make the time and do it." And he did.

Thinking that paying tribute to others isn't that big of a deal is reinforced by the fact that pretty much everyone thinks this way, too. It's just not something we normally do in our society. But *normal* doesn't necessarily equate to *healthy*. For example, it's normal for many of us to eat in a way that raises our cholesterol levels or causes diabetes, but that isn't healthy.

Just as an unhealthy lifestyle can have unintentional dire consequences, failing to express gratitude can cause you pain. So you can keep doing what's "normal," but this pain is what you have to live with when you don't try something different.

It's Never Too Soon

When I began to talk to people about my victory-lap project, I'd hear heartbreaking stories of regret again and again. This brings to mind the time I was talking to the CEO of a large European conglomerate, and I must have hit a nerve because tears welled up in his eyes.

The man proceeded to tell me that he never could have gotten into the business he was in without the first guy who'd helped him set up a manufacturing plant. Many years later the CEO heard that this road-changer wasn't doing well, but he was too busy building his multinational company to contact his old supporter. The man died, and my friend never forgave himself for this neglect.

℘ ℘ ℘

For many years, I have belonged to the Young Presidents' Organization and their men's support groups, called "forums," both on the East Coast and in Southern California. At these forums, ten or so members meet monthly for four hours; they also go away together once a year for two or three days to share business and personal experiences in an atmosphere of confidentiality, trust, and openness.

For about 25 years I was in two forums simultaneously: in Long Island, New York; and in New York City. I'm still in the New York City forum, and I've been in another one in San Diego for the past 12 years. These forums have been both a source of my own personal development as well as my opportunity to contribute to others.

In my Long Island forum, there was a fellow named Len who helped open up the group by being very vulnerable, disclosing some of the challenges he faced regarding a very significant personal issue. This encouraged others to talk at that level, too. Just as a personal expression of gratitude, I wrote a letter to Len thanking him for what he brought to the group and how much I appreciated it. Among other things, I wrote: "Your willingness to share, your warmth, your caring, and your efforts to make a difference are great gifts. Thank you for the enrichment and friendship that you are bringing to my life."

Almost a decade later, that same forum group came up with the idea that each man would introduce another by saying what that person meant to him. Len got to introduce me. Amazingly, he incorporated my letter, which, in his words, he'd "saved and cherished" for nine years! He also made his own tribute to me in the form of a letter because he said that he couldn't rely on being able to remember everything he wanted to say. I still have that letter, in which Len included these words: "I'll never forget the moment after I'd made an emotional presentation, when you embraced me with a hug that was an uninhibited expression of your affection."

Then a couple of years after that, Len dropped dead of a heart attack on the way to the dentist. He was only 54. Our group was now left with nothing but our memories and reflections of a man who was no longer there, but I had that exchange of letters between us, too. As such, I didn't feel a sense that things had been left unsaid by either of us.

Closer to home, on Lola's office wall there's a picture of a flower along with a framed handwritten letter of appreciation, which our son Jason put together for her when he was 11 years old. Right next to it, also framed, is a beautiful poem that Lola's sister, Ellen, wrote to pay tribute to their father after he died. Although I've been touched by that poem, I've more recently reflected on what this gesture might have meant to my father-in-law had he received it while he was still alive.

The tributes on my wife's wall clearly illustrate the two ways to do something. You can either choose to express your own appreciation in this moment—regardless of your age—or wait until someone you care about dies and write or say something that he or she will never get to appreciate.

The Bittersweetness of a Eulogy

The customary time for expressing our feelings about someone in our society is during a eulogy. Yet even when memorial services and funerals are done well, they're bittersweet: sweet because of the heartfelt words; bitter because the person being acknowledged is unable to hear them.

When Gary Reif, a dear friend of mine, died at the age of 57 after a six-year battle with pancreatic cancer, the funeral service was organized on very short notice. I was asked to speak, and I really wanted to pay a moving final tribute to him.

I was blessed to have been able to spend a lot of time with Gary during his protracted illness, so I'd had many opportunities to express my heartfelt appreciation to him for what he'd meant in my life. Although some others did the same, the reality is that most people at the funeral hadn't taken advantage of the opportunity to visit Gary during those difficult final years, nor did they get to speak at his funeral. For them, much remained unsaid.

I mention this story because of a remarkable man named Gordon Carrier, whom I had the good fortune to encounter just prior to Gary's memorial service. Gordon, an amazingly creative and caring human being, put together the audio and visual effects to support all aspects of the program devoted to our close friend. The style, warmth, energy, and commitment he demonstrated to make the final good-bye to Gary a very special one set a standard by which these moving events can be judged.

Gordon and I subsequently became friends. During my victory-lap conversation with him, I told him how he'd made an indelible impression on me that day; he not only showed up, but he was a leader, and I'll always be grateful to him for that. Even though he is a world-class architect and creative force, what stood out on that day (and thereafter) was his heart, character, and integrity; these qualities, complemented by his humor and flair, will always be a part of me.

❦ ❦ ❦

While I was on my gratitude journey, I was told about something that renowned columnist Art Buchwald had done, which was certainly an exception to the typical eulogy.

Art had checked into a hospice because he was terminally ill with kidney disease, and he was told to put things in order since his days were numbered. But he continued to amaze himself and others when he lived much longer than expected. A prolific author, he was afforded enough time to write another book, *Too Soon to Say Goodbye*.

Art had already picked out a number of people who he hoped would deliver eulogies at his memorial service, including broadcast journalists Tom Brokaw and Mike Wallace; former *Washington Post* editor Ben Bradlee; film producer George Stevens, Jr.; and others. When Art didn't die as anticipated, he asked these men to write their eulogies early so that he could print them at the end of his book. As Art wrote: "Instead of being memorialized after my death, I get to read what they were going to say now. It's very rare that someone has the chance to hear his own eulogies."

It's obvious that Art really enjoyed reading what his old friends had to say. And I'm sure that those who wrote them received equal satisfaction and closure from the fact that Art got to hear them.

The key here is that Art Buchwald's loved ones had the benefit of a window of opportunity in which to express everything previously left unsaid. That opportunity did not exist in the case of my friend Len, leaving those who loved him feeling bereft. I cannot think of a stronger selling point for the concept of a gratitude journey than describing it as an opportunity to seize the moment and avoid the pain of regret.

So Much Left Unsaid . . .

My own source of regret is that I never told my father and mother how much I appreciated them. I believe that these would have been profound emotional experiences. It's true that my father's death when I was 17 denied me the opportunity to discuss so much with him, including my gratitude. It's tempting to rationalize by saying, "What would I have known to say as a 17-year-old?" Then I remember what my own son was able to write to his mother at the age of 11!

On the other hand, I was so blessed to have my mother survive life-threatening bouts of breast cancer when she was 37 and 78 and then live to age 93. I wanted to capture her remarkable life and have her story preserved in her own voice, so I taped an interview with her when she was 80 years old and had her supplement this interview with a 20-page autobiography. I also spent most of the last two months of her life with her, yet I still wish that I knew then what I know now about expressing gratitude. I know she understood how much I loved and respected her, but I never was explicit in my expression of profound gratitude to her for everything she'd done for me.

For most of us, there is no more influential relationship than the one we have with our parents. If you're fortunate that your parents are still alive, you may want to initiate your own expressions of gratitude toward them. To that end, I gave some thought to what I would have said to my mother and father if only I'd taken the opportunity. My hope in doing so is that it will encourage you to think about what you appreciate about *your* parents and give you some ideas on how to frame the conversation.

I'd be less than candid if I didn't mention that writing these letters, although an emotional process, was decidedly less gratifying than if I'd been able to express my feelings to my parents when they were alive. And after having completed my journey, I really appreciate the difference. When putting these thoughts down on paper, I felt as though I were talking on the phone and the other person had been disconnected.

I know my parents didn't feel that they were missing out on anything, because it wasn't common back then (nor is it today) for sons or daughters to express these words to their parents. That's why the conversations would have been even more poignant.

Now that my mom and dad are no longer alive, I can only imagine the look in their eyes, the reaction on their faces, the feel of their presence, the warmth of their embrace, and the impact of my words. Sadly, I was unable to have the pleasure of giving this gift to them. I'm left wishing that I'd had the wisdom, foresight, and experience back then that I do today. I never would have missed this special moment to express all that they meant to me.

My Father

Fathers are a powerful force in their sons' lives. For many years, I felt deprived not only by the effects of my dad's serious heart attack when I was 11, but by his premature death. Even when Dad was alive, he was not very present in my life: our verbal communications were limited and not memorable. The reality was that my father, while comfortable conversing with others, was not much of a communicator with either my brother, Ray, or me.

Dad's passion for horses and love of adventure led him to the Adirondack Mountains, where he put his life savings into developing a dude ranch, which was a high-risk investment and big-time gamble with the family's financial resources. After three years of struggle, a major storm washed away access to the ranch, and we lost everything.

When I was a child, fathers were the providers, which reinforced their position as the rock of the family. I realize now that my mother was the foundation for most of the other areas of my life, but the importance of my father being the breadwinner was always present.

For years after Dad died, I wouldn't discuss my relationship with him with either family or friends. It was only many years later, when the topic was discussed in my forum groups, that I finally articulated my feelings. At that time, a couple of decades after his death, the remnants of my recollections were that I was a young boy who grew up fearful that my father would die at any minute, and I was constantly preoccupied with not doing anything that could accelerate his death.

My view of my dad had formed when I was a teenager and became frozen in my mind. Later it was reinforced by comparing how involved I was with my sons during their own childhoods and teen years. I'd failed to appreciate that times had changed, and back when I was a child, fathers were not as engaged with their sons as they were when I was bringing up my own boys. And I was less engaged with my sons than fathers are today. As my perspective changed, so did my memory of my dad.

It became clear to me that for years I never acknowledged my father for who he was or the impact he had on me. I've now grown a little closer to him.

Here's what I so regret never telling him:

I wish we'd spent more time together. I don't re-member even having a game of catch with you. There I go, comparing you to what my generation did when we became fathers. How unfair of me. The truth is, I did not feel shortchanged at the time.

There was a minor league baseball team in Jacksonville, and I'll never forget the few games we went to together. I wasn't really into the sport, but I loved being with you and having you all to myself. We both got excited when we saw this 19-year-old African-American player hit winning home runs. I had a deeply moving moment many years later when I went to a baseball game with my son in San Francisco. I looked out at the billboard in center field that listed the leading home-run hitters of all time, and there was that same player's name: Hank Aaron. It brought tears to my eyes when I thought back to those special times with you, Dad.

I also remember that after the baseball games, we usually went to a coffee shop for a late-night snack. I'll never forget one night when you saw two people who worked for you eating in the restaurant. You called the waiter over and said that you wanted to pay their check. It's clear that the pleasure I get to this day from doing acts of kindness is rooted in the gratitude seen in the eyes of those you treated that night.

*I learned from your friends after your death
that you not only squeezed so much out of life, you
always lived up to a very high ethical standard
as well. In the best sense of the phrase, they described you by saying, "He was a good man."*

*Dad, I had to grow up fast when I thought
that you might die young. That's not what I
would have chosen for my life, but in most
ways it has served me well. It made me focus,
be purposeful, and be grateful for every day
I have. It has also served as a vivid reminder
that life is not about what hand you're dealt,
it's all about how you play it. Nothing has been
a more profound influence on my life.*

*May you rest in peace. Know that I will never
forget you. And know that I will never get over
the loss.*

My Mother

Knowing that there was a possibility my father
may not live a long life and she'd need to have a
source of income, my mother entered the real-estate
field in her late 40s and owned a small firm until she
was 80.

She was a voracious reader from the time she was
a teenager, even starting a lending library off her back
porch when she was 13: one penny a day for a book.
She graduated at age 19 from Hunter College and

taught school for 12 years. I estimate that my mother read more than 8,000 books during her lifetime.

By most accounts, anyone being objective would say that she'd lived a tough life. Just during the course of my own life, she survived the family's financial ruin when Dad's business venture failed, had to deal with a radical mastectomy at age 37 while raising 6- and 7-year-old sons, and lived through the deaths of two husbands.

Here is some of what I regret not having said to her:

While I was growing up, you made life seem normal even though it was anything but. A case in point: When Dad died, you were left with very little financially. I was a first-semester freshman attending the University of Michigan, and the cost of that school was three times as much as the University of Florida, where I could have gone. You didn't blink when I raised the question about whether there would be enough money for me to continue at Michigan. You didn't even want me to feel that I had to work to help with expenses, but it was the least I could do. You wanted only the best for your sons, no matter what the personal sacrifice. I learned later that you'd used a substantial portion of your limited assets to keep me at school. My college life was a real life-changer for me, and I'll never forget your selflessness in making it possible.

You made the most of the better years by traveling around the world, which was documented in the multitude of photo albums and journals of these remarkable trips. My love of travel no doubt had its genesis in your sharing these mind-expanding, joyful experiences.

How proud I was that you shared your passion for books with so many people. Your annual lists of your reviews of 75 or so of the year's best and most noteworthy books were sought after by so many that I, in the role of your "publisher," insisted that people pay for them. They were happy to do so since you contributed 100 percent of the revenue to the Southside Public Library, where you volunteered your time. The library used the donations to buy more books for you to read and write about, and the cycle continued.

From observing your work at the library over the years, I saw the pleasure and meaning to be had from finding a cause that's aligned with your passion and supporting it with personal service as well as financially. It's a model that drives my philanthropy to this day.

Ray and I were so happy when you remarried Dr. Morris Myers later in life. He adored you, and you had such a blissful relationship with him. Yet as if you hadn't had enough hardships in your life, six years into that marriage, your husband became bedridden, unable to move his legs or speak. For the next

*nine-and-a-half years, you managed to care for him
in your apartment with the aid of part-time nurses.
Loyalty is one of my highest ideals, and I couldn't
have had a better role model than you.*

*At no time in your life did I ever hear you
utter a word that suggested you were a victim—
just the opposite. In your autobiography, you
wrote: "I love each day that I have. I thank
God for the wonderful life I have had and for
the blessings I've enjoyed."*

*I'll never forget the thrill and pride that I felt
when you were honored at age 93. It was the day
before you left Jacksonville to live with Ray and
[his wife] Joan in Boston during the last two
months of your life. Ray, you, and I had a meeting with the mayor of Jacksonville to accept your
award for Volunteer of the Quarter for the city.
You were later posthumously awarded the Volunteer of the Year for the thousands of dollars you
had contributed to your library from the sale of
"Sylvia's Annual Book Review." I can't imagine
the thrill you and I would have experienced if
I'd written This Is the Moment! when you were
alive. I have a feeling it would be number one
on your book list. In any case, I know Ray and I
were always number one in your eyes.*

*Your legacy of love, devotion, loyalty, and phi-
lanthropy; and your passion for travel, books, and
your family have been emblazoned on my heart*

and will be with me forever as guiding lights. Your loyalty was legendary. I could never repay you for your love and support during my formative years or for the lessons you taught me throughout my life.

No son could have loved a mother more, nor have been more loved in return.

@ @ @

Now that you know why expressing gratitude is so powerful—and why *not* expressing it can be so painful—I'm going to tell you more about some of the people who have made a difference to me. The next part of the book is all about these life-changers, and how I expressed my gratitude to them.

@ @ @ @

PART II

THE
CONVERSATIONS

CHAPTER FIVE

THE FORMATIVE YEARS

*"Feeling gratitude and not expressing it
is like wrapping a present
and not giving it."*

— WILLIAM ARTHUR WARD

My life falls roughly into three distinct phases: The first 29 years were filled with constant change in all areas. The next 29 were my building years, both personally and professionally. The current phase has been spent harvesting that which I've sowed, and it's become a time to refocus my interests toward making a difference in the lives of others.

I've decided to catalogue my 44 gratitude conversations in the same way. Thus, you'll notice that this part of the book goes through my life chronologically, allowing you to meet my life-changers in approximately the same order that I did.

First we're going to look at my formative years. During this phase of my life, I think that the major opportunities for personal growth and enrichment stemmed from struggles and losses, although I may not have recognized this at the time. I wonder what would have happened had my father—a tall, handsome Austrian immigrant with a limited grasp of English—stayed in the meatpacking field after I was born. But that wasn't in the cards; instead, he lost the dude ranch, and times got very hard for my family. My brother, Ray, and I were just four and three at the time, so the move into my grandparents' two-bedroom New York City home was hard on everyone, especially my mother.

We moved out as soon as possible, but all my parents could afford was an apartment in the tough neighborhood of Elizabeth, New Jersey. As better job opportunities opened up for my dad, we'd move again: first to Albany, New York, and then to Schenectady. Relocating to a new city every two years was hard on us kids, particularly since as soon as we'd make friends, we'd have to leave.

The constant upheaval was difficult, but not nearly as traumatic as when I was nine years old and came home from school to discover that my mother was in the hospital in need of a serious operation due to cancer. She had a radical mastectomy, and we subsequently learned that the next five years would be critical. If Mom could live until I was 14, she'd have the possibility of a long life. That five-year watch was terrifying, since she was the rock of our family.

As if my mother's health issues didn't place enough stress on the family, my father had a near-fatal heart attack when I was 11. During the ensuing years, Ray and I would repress our natural boyish tendencies to argue, and generally avoided conflict for fear of giving Dad another heart attack.

With the possibility looming that I could lose one or both of my parents any day, I took on odd jobs including paper routes, babysitting, caddying, and shoveling snow. Fortunately, I was tall for my age and could pass for three or four years older, even though I was barely a teenager.

We moved again. This time, we were off to Florida for my father's health, first to Coral Gables and then to Jacksonville. Now in the tenth grade, I continued earning money by selling ladies' shoes after school, on Saturdays, and during summers. I not only earned money, but I saved it, too. This reinforced my belief that I could manage if, God forbid, my father died. Simply put, I grew up fast.

These multiple moves, my parents' health issues, and my early working life were all maturing factors. I believe that this maturity, coupled with my physical presence, contributed to my being elected president of a prominent club in my high school at the age of 16. It was my first experience in a leadership role, and soon I had my first experience with meeting a true road-changer.

Early Influencers

During our formative years, there are often people whose influence dramatically changes the course of our lives in very important ways, either by affecting what we do or the extent to which we're able to do it. Many of us have a friend or even an acquaintance, sometimes met by chance, who has had a profound influence on our life. It's most likely that person about whom we say, "If it hadn't been for . . ." Often, though, we lose touch with these individuals as we all get on with our lives. Tracking them down can be enormously gratifying, made easier today with modern communications technology.

Luckily for me, I maintained my relationship with this particular road-changer over the decades, giving us a multitude of shared moments, a history, and traditions that are irreplaceable.

A True Road-Changer

After high school, I initially planned to attend the University of Florida. Then by chance I met someone who changed my mind about this decision, and he changed my *life* in profound ways, too.

A senior at the University of Michigan, Harry Gaines convinced me that an education there would be a far better learning experience. I was accepted, and a few months later I drove with my new friend to the campus in Ann Arbor—a thousand miles from home and a place I'd never been to before—to commence my freshman year. Harry also encouraged me to join a particular fraternity. Both of these were pivotal events for me.

This particular relationship goes long and deep, since I've known Harry since I was 17. We've always been there for each other in times of need, and we've shared many great times over the years as well. Here is an excerpt from my conversation with him:

You've had such a big, big impact on my life. If I'd never spent another hour with you after the age of 22, you'd still have had a profound influence on me. But you've been there at many life-changing experiences over the years, and no one could have had a better man in his corner.

You were always nurturing and encouraging me. I see a central theme of loyalty, education, and wanting the best for me. No matter what the crisis was, you were powerful in your presence. You were always there. You were extraordinary in getting me to places I wouldn't have gotten to, but also in keeping me from going down for the count on occasion.

Of all my dear friendships, no one has been through so many of my highs and lows as you have. I have loved the many good times we've shared; but I'll never forget the advice, comfort, and support you gave me during the difficult moments.

Three months into my freshman year, I got a phone call telling me that my dad was ill and I needed to go home. I arrived back that same day to discover that he'd already died. My greatest fear had now become a reality. At my mom's urging, I returned to school, but it was a hard decision to leave her to deal with the grief and loss. In this tough time, Harry was there to offer me comfort, support, and guidance. Again, I consider myself so fortunate to have always had such an amazing friend in my corner.

Q Q Q

In my junior year, I was elected president of my fraternity. My size, stature, prior work experiences, and coping skills learned from dealing with my father's death played a role in my getting elected; as did having led a high-school club. Heading this group of exceptional people was another great learning and leadership opportunity for me.

I graduated in four years with a bachelor's degree in business administration, with an emphasis in accounting. Considering my less-than-ideal high-school education in Jacksonville; the competitive nature of the academic program at Michigan; the huge personal challenge I faced during my freshman year; and my extracurricular activities, including being president of the fraternity, this was no small achievement for me.

A six-month stint in the Army at Fort Jackson in Columbia, South Carolina, followed. After the military, returning to Jacksonville would have been the most likely path for me. Yet I chose to accept a position with a company owned by the father of one of my fraternity brothers. He hired me to sell rags—euphemistically called "industrial textiles"—out of Pittsburgh. I put my all of my possessions in my car and went off to the local YMCA, where I stayed until I moved in to a shared place with three strangers.

The job did not work for me on several levels, nor was this living situation what I'd envisioned for myself, so I took a job with a certified public accounting firm in Cambridge, Massachusetts. I stayed for three years, which was a requirement for becoming a CPA. I had no intentions of remaining in the field, but for me it was the equivalent of going to graduate school, and I was almost able to make a living. To earn extra money, I sold mutual funds in the evenings.

Then came what turned out to be another early defining moment, which arrived courtesy of my older brother, Ray.

The Big Brother

The relationship between siblings is unique in both its length and its importance, and having one or both parents in common creates another bond. Our brothers and sisters often significantly color our lives, be it during childhood or later when we're adults; however, until we really give it some thought, we often take these relationships for granted. When I took the time to reflect on it, I realized that my own brother had greatly impacted my life, although not always in the way I expected at the time.

Ray had told me that he'd made a thousand dollars in one month, and only working part-time, by selling a vitamin-and-mineral supplement called NutriBio. That was more money than I was making from both of my jobs combined, so I sent him $500 for inventory and became part of a sales pyramid.

The inventory took up most of the room in my tiny studio apartment. Realizing I had to build a sales organization fast, I put up a notice in the Laundromat I frequented to solicit salespeople. I got an immediate response and hired my first salesperson. Unfortunately, shortly thereafter the FDA shut down NutriBio for making unsubstantiated claims about its pills.

It was the biggest financial loss of my early life, but it was also the biggest gain. Lola, the only person I'd hired, became my wife 20 months later when I was 24. Without a doubt, it was the best decision I ever made.

Although Ray and I have not been geographically close over the years, we've worked hard to stay in touch. We became much closer after working together to manage our mother's last three months. Here's some of what he inspired me to say:

During our challenging childhoods, you were a very important person to me and a stabilizing force. I can't imagine what that early stage of my life would have been like without you.

Although our college choices took us to very different places, we did not grow apart. You've been incredibly supportive, especially at the crucial turning points of my life. Even unintentionally, you've brought me great happiness: without your NutriBio business opportunity, there was no way I'd ever have met my Lola.

You not only set a standard for hard work and personal discipline, but you were also someone I could always count on.

I love seeing you play the role of patriarch with your children and extended family. Your competence and aptitude toward business is second to none. All of this has been achieved with a strong moral compass that has guided you in both your personal and business lives.

It's been reassuring having your presence throughout my life. Our mother would be so proud of both of our successes and, even more important, how close we've become.

When recognizing the role of my brother in my life, I have to also acknowledge his wife of 30 years. Joan has not only enriched his life but added immeasurably to the connectedness of all our family; she could not have been better to my mother had she been her own daughter. Joan is quietly competent in whatever she does.

Life Enhancers

Within days of becoming a CPA, I left public accounting. Over the next few years I got my first introduction into the hospitality business: following six months at a Boston hotel as a controller, I was transferred to the same position at the Royal Orleans Hotel in New Orleans.

When I thought about those early years, I began to notice that there were people who had enhanced my life, not necessarily by influencing what I did, but through the qualities they brought to it. These individuals had brought me joy, personal fulfillment, and peace of mind.

The Lover of Life

We all have people in our lives whose very presence makes our days brighter and more joyful just by the way they experience the world. My old friend Denny Davis, whom I've known since my days in New Orleans, is one of these. He remained in the hospitality industry until he retired and now lives close to me in Southern California.

These words capture only a fraction of the fondness I have for Denny:

Your humor, your love of life, and your capacity to make the best out of any situation are just a few of your extraordinary qualities that made an indelible impression on me. What I love about our friendship is that you're a brilliant model for not taking life too seriously, a person who loves life regardless of what it throws at him.

Although you're able to tell a funny story in such a way that it's like riding a wave of happiness and joy, you're also informed and present when it comes to having conversations about more serious issues.

I treasure how close you are to my son Jonathan. You know how I feel about my family, and by showing the interest and warmth for my son, you further magnify my affection for you.

After New Orleans I was recruited as the administrative vice president of a 60-restaurant chain in New York City. Lola and I made this move when she was in an advanced stage of pregnancy. A month or so later, to our surprise (and even to our doctor's!), Lola delivered twin boys: Jonathan and Jason.

Our life was again redefined when I was recruited to become controller of a start-up company in the newly emerging executive conference center field. I invested my life savings of $10,000 in return for a very small percentage of ownership in the company.

During these years of building up Harrison Conference Centers, I developed a strong interest in education, and that's when Hal Lazarus came into my life.

The Eternal Optimist

Hal has been teaching for more than 50 years, and he also served as dean of the business school at Hofstra University. It was Hal who introduced me to teaching, which became an important dimension in my life. What makes this contribution so remarkable is that it has provided a lifetime of fulfillment for me.

Like Denny Davis, Hal Lazarus is a lover of life. A few years ago, he lost his arm to cancer. When I asked him what his greatest challenge was, he said that it was tying his skates when he goes ice-skating! I wondered how he coped, and he said that he asked the person next to him to help. No big deal. Hal's vocabulary does not include the word *victim*. These traits are highlighted in my tribute to him:

> *You introduced me to the world of teaching by inviting me to be a guest lecturer at your graduate business-school classes. That was an important contribution to me because I think there's a teacher in me, and you gave me an opportunity to mine that capacity. I'm very grateful for that.*

You also exposed me to publishing by doing the joint study on meeting effectiveness with Hofstra University.

Even more important, you were always an enthusiastic supporter of so many of my endeavors, not to mention those of my family.

You never really need a party to create a good time. You're basically a "make happy" kind of person. There doesn't seem to be anything that cracks that optimism and joyfulness of yours. Perhaps the biggest lesson I learned from you is your positive attitude in life, no matter what the challenges.

The Peace-of-Mind Giver

With the help of Lola's parents, we bought our first home for our young family just five minutes from Harrison's corporate offices in Glen Cove, Long Island. Along with investing our life savings in the company, this was another maturing event. At this time in our lives, we felt vulnerable and, yes, maybe even a little frightened. It was important to have people around who eased our anxiety and helped us get through this uncertain time. That's where Jerry DeSimone comes in.

Jerry was my insurance advisor, whom I met when our twins were very young and I carried the fear of dying young like my father. He went on to become a dear friend, as the paragraphs that follow detail:

By your helping me secure significant life insurance as well as an investment in real estate on our sons' behalf years ago, I was reassured that my family would be taken care of financially in the event of my premature death. At the time, I thought if I lived long enough, I might be able to provide for the family; however, if I had a heart attack like my father, then my wife and two little kids were in trouble. I want to make sure you understand that the peace of mind that came from knowing that I'd taken care of my wife and kids was all due to you.

In addition, your advice on my company matters over the years, including all aspects of employee benefits, was invaluable.

What transcended these important contributions, however, was having such a caring and thoughtful person with my interests and those of my family always paramount to him. What has impressed me is not only what you've done for me but how you've done it. You could not have done any more for me if I were part of your family. You were always wanting the best and making sure I did not spend a cent more than necessary.

The Good Doctor

There has never been anything more important to me than maintaining great health, because without it nothing else is possible. For some three decades, Chuck Heilbrunn was our family doctor, and to this day he remains a very close personal friend:

Chuck, your friendship was so multifaceted. You were my favorite tennis mate, a source of innumerable deep and meaningful conversations, and a very caring and competent internist, to name just a few of the dimensions of our relationship.

You cannot imagine how much you affected my life just by knowing that you were there for me, Lola, and the boys 24/7. Quite simply, you treated us as your own family. Whether it was sports injuries; occasional minor surgeries; or, of course, my periodic concerns about my heart, you were always there, always concerned, and always helpful.

Our family could not have been luckier to have such a compassionate and knowledgeable doctor. This good fortune could only be equaled by having your loyalty, support, and friendship over all these years.

What could be more important than having good health and deep friendship, all wrapped in one relationship? I have indeed been blessed by your presence in my life.

@ @ @

Glen Cove was the 14th city I'd lived in, and the site of my 14th job, all in only 29 years. For the first time, I had high hopes that my life was going to have some stability, and that my desire for developing meaningful personal friendships would now be possible. Lola was totally supportive of my intense focus on making Harrison Conference Centers successful in spite of the demands of raising our twin sons without assistance (except from me for a couple hours in the evenings and on weekends).

This brings me to the next part of my life story: the building years.

@ @ @ @ @

CHAPTER SIX

THE BUILDING YEARS

"Appreciation is a wonderful thing.
It makes what is excellent in others
belong to us as well."

— VOLTAIRE

The next phase of my life encompasses the building years, spanning from the time I invested my savings in Harrison Conference Centers to when I sold the company 29 years later.

When I first began to work at Harrison, I could not have anticipated that this pathfinding, start-up company would be out of cash and near bankruptcy within three years. Nor could I have foreseen what happened next.

The two founders, who were also the president and the chairman of the company, were asked to leave. Although I was only 32, I was made president of the

400-employee business, and then six months later became its chairman and CEO, titles I would hold for the next 25 years. During this time, ownership shifted from primarily institutional owners to me and my senior management team.

Looking back on those years now, I can't help but think how similar my choices were to those my father made. Upon reflection, I see that we shared something else in common: We were dreamers. We both left relatively safe, traditional areas to put our life savings into high-risk start-up businesses in the hospitality field. In my case it was even riskier than Dad's because he owned his business, whereas I was only able to acquire a very small interest in mine. And we both did it when we had two small sons (although we also had the blessing of a supportive wife).

After three years, my father's dude ranch and the family were bankrupt. Thirty years later, Harrison Conference Centers was facing the same fate at the three-year mark, and I was looking at the prospect of losing my savings. Dad and I both worked really hard, and fortunately my story had a much better outcome.

It's clear to me that due to the support and guidance offered by the many men and women I later thanked on my victory lap, I was able to navigate life more successfully than my father did. I can only presume that it would have helped him to have the kind of personal resources I've had, but that's only conjecture on my part.

Agents of Change

Those special people who teach us something that changes the way we look at and approach life, or how we make things happen, can greatly impact our lives. I'm not talking about becoming competent in one situation or handling a specific problem; rather, it's like having a tool set that helps us in a variety of situations and has long-term benefits.

The tools could have been given to us early in life by a teacher, a professor, a colleague, or a mentor; we might even get them from a book or a seminar we attended. I received mine from Dr. Fred Jervis. I will always be grateful to Michael Kay, who introduced Fred to me.

Of all the people on my yearlong journey, Michael was the only one I worked with at two different companies. When we were in our late 20s, we were both members of the management team at the Royal Orleans Hotel in New Orleans; then, shortly after I joined Harrison, I recruited him for a management position.

In both of these jobs I learned from Michael, but the greatest contribution to my life was when he mentioned that he'd worked with a Fred Jervis, whom he'd found to be a remarkable, brilliant thinker. Michael encouraged me to reach out to him, and I'm so glad I did.

The Unique Thinker

Fred Jervis is the founder of the Center for Constructive Change, which he ran for 35 years. His firm has helped thousands of individuals and many for-profit and nonprofit organizations achieve extraordinary results.

I attended a seminar Fred taught, and it was life-changing. His unique way of constructing a framework for managing change is so profound that it's influenced all areas of my life, along with the lives of those I've coached over the years.

Fred was blinded in World War II when he was just 19. I asked him once what the major impact of this was, and he replied that his blindness not only led him to his profession, but he also felt that it gave him an edge. Since he was unable to make visual observations, he'd developed a remarkable ability to ask questions that helped his clients clarify their purpose and achieve their hoped-for results.

Fred is 87 years old now, so my visit with him at his home in New Hampshire was extra special. (I would be remiss if I didn't mention the added pleasure of seeing Jan, Fred's business partner and wife of 60-plus years, before our meeting.) Here's some of what I told him:

> *Over a 35-year period, we worked together on many occasions. Your unique way of thinking and creating positive outcomes has profoundly influenced all areas of my personal and professional life in thousands of ways.*

I know you've influenced a lot of people, but just from my perspective, I want you to understand that not a day goes by that I don't marvel in some way at the process of thinking that you brought to my life. I came here to tell you from the deepest places in my heart and my head and my soul how fortunate I've felt to have met you. I'm so indebted to you for what you've done for me, and I want to let you know that when I'm helping others, it's paying forward what I've learned from you over these many years.

I'm not only eternally grateful for your contribution to my life, but also for those I care about and whom I've now been able to help. I cannot adequately express how profound an impact you've had on my life, and I thank you so very, very much for it.

Business Blessings

How can we adequately express gratitude to someone who made a financial contribution or investment that enabled our dreams to come true? It might have been a grandparent who paid our college tuition or an investor who helped us grow our small business.

When someone supports you with that type of commitment because he or she cares about what you're doing, that individual then becomes an integral part of how things play out in your life. Russ Carson was such a person for me.

The Two-Generational Supporter

Russ and I go back to the earliest days of my career with Harrison Conference Centers. When we first met, he'd just joined Citibank Venture Capital, and Harrison was his first investment. He became a member of our board of directors and remained on it for more than a decade. After Citibank, he became a founder and general partner of what became a major private-equity investment firm. Years later, Russ hired my son Jason as a summer employee and ever since has remained a supporter, as you can tell from the paragraphs that follow:

> *Even though you were early in your career when you were on our board, you fully understood the nature of the relationship between company management and its investors. It's never a simple one, and it's made even more difficult when it's a start-up company in a new industry. Russ, you were unique. You never used your position to usurp the responsibilities of the management of our company, even during difficult times. Quite the contrary—your wisdom, judgment, clarity, constructive insights, and support were both invaluable and refreshing. I always felt that you were a cheerleader in both acknowledging accomplishments and inspiring new initiatives. I'll never forget your presence and your contribution.*
>
> *If that weren't enough, you were an inspiration and mentor to my son Jason and now an investor in his venture-capital firm.*

It was a real blessing to have had such a supportive business investor for so many years. It's unique when that person influences two generations of the same family in two very different industries, and for that I am doubly grateful.

The Trusted Colleague

In any vocation, our success is usually a direct reflection of the quality of the people we work with and their capacity to complement each other and collaborate. Whether we work for them or they work for us, it has a tremendous effect on how well we do. Unfortunately, too often we don't fully appreciate the importance of the roles these colleagues can play in our lives.

During the building years of my life, I was fortunate to have the support and dedication of hundreds of talented and committed employees, and they were critical to the survival of Harrison Conference Centers in the early years and to its success thereafter. These were people whose unique skills, competency, commitment, and teamwork were essential to my business achievements.

I could not have been more proud of the way Harrison became the leader in the executive conference center industry. Innovative sales and operating management programs, coupled with the pursuit of excellence, were the underpinnings of our success.

No one played a more important role in Harrison's accomplishments than Jack Kealey, my business colleague for 23 years. I'm so glad I was able to let him know:

A key objective of my business life was to make Harrison the leader in its field, and I'm deeply indebted to you for your contributions to making that a reality. You created an industry-leading sales and marketing team that was the standard that others were judged by. Your programs were innovative, trailblazing, professional, and highly effective.

What made your contribution exceptional was that after having proven your programs (such as consultative selling and quality assurance) in your division, you introduced them throughout our entire organization. The trust that you earned over the years was based on the fact that you were a straight shooter and always had the best interests of the company at heart. I had a high level of personal involvement with our sales organization due to your initiative in making it happen, for which I'm very grateful.

I also cherished that you always brought your heart and great people skills to all situations.

I'm deeply indebted to you for your support over our years together and your continuing leadership of Harrison after I sold the company.

The Steadfast Aide-de-Camp

Grace Jara was my administrative assistant for 25 years. When she joined us at Harrison, she was in her mid-40s and one of the most experienced and mature staff members at our young company. Shortly after coming to work with us, her husband died, leaving her with five children to raise. She remained strong, and remarkably this tragedy didn't diminish her effectiveness and commitment to me and my company. She's a truly amazing woman and will always be in my life and my heart:

I could not have had a more competent, loyal, hardworking, committed, and diplomatic assistant. You were really cool under pressure, even when I was unreasonable in my demands to have it "just right." It was never a problem for you because you also wanted the same thing. The level of perfection we wanted and the long hours we worked were routine, but you never got flustered. I might have gotten upset a time or two, but you stayed calm and collected.

We did an enormous amount of work over 25 years, under varying but often difficult conditions. You had maturity, good judgment, and a gift of common sense; and you provided an ever-present sounding board for me. Bottom line: I could always count on you for extraordinary performance far outside the confines of even the broadest definition of an administrative assistant. And we had fun in the process!

Grace, you've been a remarkable influence on my life. Through all of the tough times, you were a source of strength and comfort. Simply said, you contributed in a profound way to the effectiveness and gratification of both my professional and personal lives. I'll be forever grateful to you, and I love you.

The Design Mind

Organizations often have to outsource services that can best be provided by others. As individuals, we also have to engage people who have the expertise we don't have. These services may either be provided by an individual or a company, but in any event, they're outside of our organization and have different priorities. But when they go above and beyond what we could have expected from them, and we feel that we couldn't have accomplished what we did without them, that's something extraordinary.

Harrison Conference Centers had state-of-the-art meeting rooms, not to mention first-class guest accommodations and dining and recreational facilities. That's largely due to Bob Hillier, one of the leading architects in the United States, and his firm, who were actively involved in the design of several of our centers.

Although we'd spoken a few times, Bob and I hadn't seen each other in ten years when we sat down to talk. Our infrequent communication didn't diminish my enormous level of appreciation and respect for him, as you can tell from the words below:

> *My own aptitude was more on the people side, and I was less capable of creating what I'd envisioned in regard to the physical spaces. I would tell you the feeling I wanted, but had no idea how to get there. Your presence was absolutely essential, as you knew what I was trying to achieve. No one did more to design and create these facilities that set the benchmark for the industry than you.*
>
> *Equally remarkable was how you did it. For over the quarter of a century that we worked together, you were always accessible, brilliantly creative, value and cost sensitive, and a consensus builder; and you delivered more than you promised. You shared my enthusiasm and were really excited about the projects. Also, you were extremely loyal, and I trusted you implicitly. Even though we didn't own anything in one another's businesses, I always felt you were just like a partner.*
>
> *You were not just a provider of architectural services; you were a friend. I'll be forever grateful to you for that.*

Networking and Human Resources

One definite advantage I had at Harrison was being associated with a group of people who were instrumental in making both my business and my life better.

Early on I realized that in order to run my company effectively, I'd need to enhance my leadership and management skills. To that end, I joined the Young Presidents' Organization (YPO) when I was in my mid-30s.

YPO is a worldwide group that provides networking opportunities for young business leaders and promotes the exchange of ideas and experiences. They offer regional, national, and international conferences that introduce members to both outstanding educational resources as well as some of the most accomplished businesspeople around the world.

Meeting Steve Ross when we were in this group together about 25 years ago was another life-changing event for me. Over the years that we've been friends, I've developed enormous respect and learned a lot from him.

Steve has been the most vivid example of someone who, when faced with highs and lows in his business and personal life, has been able to marshal internal strength and self-confidence. These factors, coupled with his sense of timing, have helped him not only survive but also achieve new heights. Steve's capabilities are evidenced by his now being one of the most successful real-estate developers in the world, along with his other varied and considerable business and philanthropic initiatives. For example, you might know him as the owner of the Miami Dolphins football team.

Steve was the one who urged me to join his YPO forum group and become its moderator, and you can be sure that I expressed my gratitude for this when we had our conversation. Over the last quarter of a century, this affiliation has been an invaluable and enriching part of both my professional and personal life, and I'll always be so grateful to him for this introduction.

It's been my experience that forum members will do anything to be supportive of each other in whatever way they can. At last count, in the three forums I've been involved with, I've attended more than 600 monthly sessions and attended around 60 annual summer conferences. These provided a great sounding board for a young president, as well as the opportunity to fine-tune my moderating skills.

These forums have also been a source of long-term relationships: guys I could call on for anything I needed. I'd like to share a little about a few of them with you now.

The Ultimate Connector

If we're really fortunate, there's a close friend we can walk every step of the way through life with, or at least a great many of these steps. I think of it as the difference between watching a movie alone or with another person: you could do it by yourself, but it's a lot more fun and interesting when you have someone to share it with. Tommy Schulhof is that guy for me.

Tommy's worldwide business operations take him frequently to China and Europe, but that does not interfere with our daily phone calls. Many business-people devote themselves to doing well in their careers so that they can then do good. Tommy's business, a clear leader in its industry, is by its very nature doing good by being an effective vehicle to help hundreds of leading nonprofits raise hundreds of millions of dollars.

Here's an excerpt from our conversation:

I'm thrilled to celebrate our relationship, which runs wide and deep. Tommy, one of the unique benefits of my relationship with you is that we share life almost in real time, or practically as it happens. Our daily calls allow me to be in the moment, whether we're addressing a major event of the day or a personal suggestion of how to make life easier or more fulfilling.

You're able to adjust the length of our conversations based on the scope of the issue, its importance in our lives, and our competing demands. Knowing that I'll speak to you sometime during the day gives me a personal sounding board of inestimable value. Whatever the source, it has created a very special friendship and bond that's filled with humor, wisdom, and deep affection.

I'm so grateful to you for the meaning, richness, joy, and laughter that you've added to my life.

The Gifted Wordsmith

Some people have a knack for describing what's happening in a way that increases our capacity to enjoy the experience, perhaps through a talent such as writing, art, or photography. One of my prized relationships is with Stephen Miron, who presents the world to me in ways that enrich my life.

Stephen is hands down one of the best-read and most capable men I know when it comes to the written word. I would have thought that this eloquence could only be honed by working as a literary critic, a professor of literature, or a screenwriter. But what makes Stephen's competency even more remarkable is that he's a businessman whose various enterprises include everything from construction materials to real-estate development and even a wine shop. As I told him:

> *Ideas, words, wine, and loyalty abound in your life. I marvel at any one of these competencies, but the sum total of them is a thing of beauty. One of the things I have a great appreciation for is your capacity to take language and make it purposeful and so alive. You can capture something on paper that just elevates the conversation. For more than two decades, I've been the beneficiary of these remarkable talents, and they have enriched my life—for which I'm so very grateful.*

The Brilliant Mind

When life comes at us, we want someone there who has the ability to take out all of the noise, get to the core issue, and then be really helpful. Similarly, with so many complicated things going on in the world, those individuals who can sort them out for us and put them in a context that makes sense are the ones who greatly enhance our life. Howard Milstein does that for me.

Howard received an undergraduate degree at Cornell and then a joint degree from Harvard Law School and Harvard Business School. Although he comes from a well-known New York real-estate family, he has used that platform to build an even larger and more successful enterprise, which includes banking, real estate, and a partnership with legendary golfer Jack Nicklaus. Here's a guy who exercises daily and listens to Aristotle and other great thinkers while he's on the treadmill:

The first thing that comes to mind when I think of you is your remarkable intellect. You're not just a smart businessman; you're equally expansive in your thinking about world affairs, politics, and philanthropy. And you just move from one to the other with great ease. I've been the beneficiary of the breadth and depth of this extraordinary intellect, which you always communicate so persuasively.

In meetings you'll cut through to the heart of a subject, serve up an assessment of it, and make a thoughtful and insightful recommendation. I have to say that's a great gift to our forum group and to me personally. I've enjoyed that quality and benefited from it on many occasions.

In addition to your business achievements, you touch all of the life's true priorities: learning; philanthropy; health; your old valued friends; and, most important, your family.

I want you to know how grateful I am for the multitude of ways you've influenced my life and the peace of mind I feel knowing that you're in my corner.

℘ ℘ ℘

During these building years, I began to realize that I'd outlived my dad.

I'd always been trying to "beat the clock," fearful that my life would be cut short, as his was at age 53. I worked out regularly and stayed in shape to minimize the prospect of an early death. When faced with the choice of taking escalators or stairs, some people choose escalators for speed and to save effort; others choose stairs for exercise. Well, I must confess that my approach toward life has always led me to jog up escalators.

Even so, now that I was in my 50s, I thought that if there were other things I wanted to do, this was the time to start doing them. Lola and I reflected on what we'd ideally like to have happen during the rest of our lives, and in light of the conclusions we came to, I sold the company, and we transplanted ourselves to California in 1998. The third phase of my life had begun.

CHAPTER SEVEN

THE REFOCUSING YEARS

*"Gratitude is not only the greatest of virtues,
but the parent of all others."*

— CICERO

Selling Harrison Conference Centers and moving to California wasn't a difficult decision for my wife and me. Lola had long dreamed about living there, and we'd both appreciated the more relaxed lifestyle on our frequent travels to the area. Plus, one of our sons had already moved to California, and the other was likely to follow suit. I realized I'd be far from my important East Coast relationships, but I intended to stay connected to them while I attempted to create some new ones on the West Coast.

This move was certainly an adventure: In the area we chose to settle, we had no friends, no work, no kids in school, no anything. Essentially, we had a clean slate. Almost immediately, I felt prompted to ask myself one of those defining questions I'd learned from Fred Jervis: *If I positioned myself to lead a meaningful life over the next five years, what would be happening in all of the important areas?*

I separated my responses into what I call "key result areas," which included personal relationships, physical health, serving the community, spirituality, financial considerations, and so forth. This process has driven my whole adult life: Thinking in terms of ideal outcomes or key results, along with indicators and benchmarks, stimulates creativity and helps me stay focused and intentional. Quite remarkably, it also provides me with a sense of freedom, since I know that my activities will be aligned with the life I ideally want to live.

So out of that process came the clarity that much of my interest centered on staying healthy, maintaining relationships, and serving others. It also became apparent that the next phase of life in our new home was to be anything but business, since I'd been working since I was a teenager. I didn't necessarily make the decision to no longer work, but when I went through this process, it simply fell off the page. That's why I've spent the last decade or so continuing with my forum groups and working with select nonprofits involved in causes that I'm passionate about, and why I've devoted an increasing amount of time to mentoring young adults.

I had an extremely gratifying and fulfilling career pioneering the executive conference center industry. But the personal satisfaction and meaning I have received from my various activities during this "refocusing phase" has surpassed the joy I experienced in business. I've often said that I wouldn't trade these last ten years for any decade of my professional life.

The Purpose Players

Even after I sold my company, my forum groups remained a very important part of my life. As I mentioned previously, I'm still active in two of them (in New York City and in San Diego), and they remain my human-relationship "laboratories." I'm close to all of the forum members, and there is no limit to what we would do for each other, both inside and outside our meetings. In many ways we treat each other as if we were close friends, and in some cases, we are just that. These are people who have enhanced my journey from success to significance.

Speaking of significance—has anybody literally saved your life? An emergency-room doctor, a firefighter, or a lifeguard might immediately spring to mind. You may have considered that these people are "just doing their job," but without them you wouldn't be here.

Such an individual might also have been a friend who warned you about an oncoming car, gave you the Heimlich maneuver, or put you in touch with a support group or resources that provided you with the critical information and direction you needed. For me, that person is Jeff Stiefler.

The Lifesaver

I met Jeff, a former president of American Express, at a conference 20 years ago. We lost touch for a while but then reconnected when he moved to Southern California a decade later. Earlier in the book, I mentioned how he helped me in the middle of the Mediterranean when I had my strangulated hernia. Here's how I articulated the gratitude I felt for him:

> *I'm so pleased to be able to express my deep appreciation for our special friendship. I know of no one who has better modeled the capacity for extraordinary positive change in all aspects of one's life.*
>
> *The blazing insight and analysis that you bring to situations, plus your ability to convey them, have enhanced my life and the lives of many others as well. I marvel at all the hours we've had in forum meetings where you've been looked at as a brilliant, funny, and profound thinker.*
>
> *I'll never forget your amazing act of friendship when I was in need of immediate surgery on the island of Corsica. Leaving your wife on the ship, waiting until I'd been operated on, and then taking*

a plane to catch up with her went above and beyond. I've never been one to reach out and ask for help, and I'm not proud of that quality. But there wasn't even a moment of hesitation on your part; you just did it. You were a source of incredible assistance and support for Lola and me during this life-threatening situation. It's hard to imagine how we could have made it without you, and I'll never forget it. I want you to know that I perceive in you that capacity for deep giving and compassion.

For all these reasons, and many more, I'm truly blessed by our friendship.

The Go-to Guy

Through our life experiences, we all acquire certain skills and information. But sometimes we need help finding a solution to a problem that falls outside of our particular area of expertise. That's when we need those people who can provide us with a body of knowledge or resources that we never would have been able to access on our own. This can be a life-altering gift for us or someone close to us. In my own life, I'm automatically reminded of Ken Hamlet.

Ken has had a stellar business career in a variety of companies and industries, from hotels (he's a past president and CEO of Holiday Inns, Inc.) to education companies to real-estate development to private equity firms. As I let him know:

Two qualities jump out at me when I think about you. One is that you're an independent thinker: the person who always offers the most unusual approach to an issue. You're infrequently in the majority, yet often it's your different point of view that turns out to be the most effective.

The second is that you're one of the world's great networkers. Over your lifetime, you've built an extraordinary contact list of the top people in your fields of interest. What's so remarkable about you is your kindness and generosity in sharing those high-level connections. When my brother was faced with a serious medical issue, for instance, you didn't hesitate to offer up all your resources for him to get the best possible advice and counsel.

Quite simply, you're a treasured friend and a "go-to guy." I look forward to the next phase of life with you because our interactions have always been exciting, interesting, stimulating, and fun.

The Facilitator

How invaluable is it when people make us more competent, teaching us how to fish, if you will, by giving us a skill that stays with us forever? Perhaps they shared an approach to life that has made us more productive, or given us pleasure in a certain area. Or maybe they listen empathetically and then ask great questions, which helps us attain clarity, focus, and resolution. They may have taught it in one evening, or they may have instructed us over the course of a semester. But once we acquired that aptitude, it stayed with us for the rest of our life.

James Newton worked in the human-development field for more than 30 years, conducting personal-growth seminars and consulting on personal and organizational change. This is what he taught me:

> *In my 35 years in forums, I was never so blessed as when the moderator role was transferred from me to you. Not only did I appreciate my new role as a participant, but I was able to learn from you as well. You are an extraordinary resource and a marvelous teacher.*
>
> *Because of your wealth of knowledge about human behavior, you were able to work at a more intense emotional level with people—you were more willing to dig deep. By observing you, I acquired important tools and approaches to life that have been enriching both personally and professionally. I distilled things that have been guiding principles for me and enlargements of my own thinking.*

Getting as Much as You Give

On rare occasions, my fellow forum members and I allow ourselves to let each other know about a particular philanthropic interest that's very important to one of us and has a specific need. Most people wouldn't do this more than once every few years; I've done it only once, period. And that was for the Elementary Institute of Science (EIS) in San Diego.

Shortly after we moved to Southern California, Lola and I were watching a morning TV show when we saw what couldn't have been more than a 60-second spot about EIS. We learned that they provide after-school, Saturday, and summer programs for children from 7 to 13 years of age in the under-served neighborhoods of southeast San Diego. We were touched by these kids, whose big eyes were filled with excitement about the hands-on science and technology experiences they were having.

I quickly ran to get a pen to write down the institute's contact information, and then I called and said that my wife and I would like to come over. I was hardly familiar with San Diego at the time, but within a day or two, Lola and I were navigating our way around and looking for the EIS building. It turned out to be a modest white house with bars on the windows.

I hadn't worked with children this age before—nor, for that matter, in the sciences. But my career had been about creating environments for learning, so the idea that EIS was education related made me feel a little bit at home. And as soon as I felt the commitment from the people there—both the staff and the kids—I became passionate about my involvement as well.

When I paid my first visit to that white house, I found out that EIS was operating on an annual budget of $175,000. Nevertheless, they had grand plans to raise an astonishing $6.5 million to tear down their 2,200-square-foot building, which had been their home for 35 years, and build a 15,000-square-foot state-of-the-art facility. After an incredible five-year effort, they were very close to doing so.

EIS leaders had applied for a $250,000 grant from the Kresge Foundation to take them to their target, but they would only qualify for it if they raised the full balance of $6.25 million. Unfortunately, they were falling a little short of that number, and just days away from the deadline to secure the grant, they'd exhausted all sources of solicitations. That's when I chose to make my forum brothers aware of the dilemma.

I sent word to the New York group, and their generosity made it possible for EIS to cross the finish line in the nick of time. What a thrilling moment that was! The institute's new facility is truly world class. In addition, they're now able to offer programs for older students, ages 14 to 17, which are just as innovative and effective as the ones for younger kids.

Although it might seem that EIS was the sole beneficiary of this generosity, understand that those who engage in any form of giving get a lot from it, too. We don't tend to fully appreciate how much *we* receive from what we originally think of as an act of kindness, generosity, or volunteerism on our part. We often think of giving as a "give up" or a "give away," but in reality, it's just as likely to be a "get." For me, nobody personifies this more than Doris Anderson.

The Bright Light

Doris, the executive director of EIS, is a remarkable woman. Her leadership and her soul have been real blessings for this institution for the past two decades. Conscious gratitude is part of her DNA, so she totally understood my victory lap. Here is an excerpt from our conversation:

> *It's pure joy to share my journey with you and to have the opportunity to express my profound gratitude for your contributions to my life. From our initial meeting, you fully grasped what I was seeking, and you delivered it in spades.*
>
> *You understood that for me, writing a check without having a personal involvement was not an option. You also didn't urge me to join your board. Instead, you gave me the title of "ambassador," and that allowed me to really identify and engage in areas where I felt I could make the biggest contribution. I'm so grateful for your wisdom in designing my involvement the way you did. It was made-to-order philanthropy for me.*
>
> *Thanks to your leadership and creativity, I've been engaged in important and meaningful ways, and it has been been richly rewarding.*

Yours is a quiet touch. You're clear on what you need, but you don't ever put anyone in a position where it looks like they can either disappoint themselves or you. You just kind of tee it up, make them aware, connect with their heart, and allow them to respond.

Not only is EIS blessed to have you as its leader, but I'm equally fortunate to have you in my life.

The Next Generation

Throughout my working life and in my forum groups, I've always tried to be a catalyst to help people be the best they can be. These years of experience have naturally extended into my involvement in mentoring the next generation. Sharing my own experiences with younger men and women, as well as asking them questions that I would have asked myself if I'd been smart enough when I was starting out, are two of the processes that seem most helpful. I know it's usually assumed that mentors have all the answers, but I work hard at making sure I have the right *questions*.

Mentors play a key role in the lives of young adults, since their parents have most likely transitioned out of that aspect of the parenting role. Mentors don't compete with or preempt the parents' role; just the opposite. Mentors are complementary to mothers and fathers, as they can bring new ideas and experiences to kids without the baggage of history present in all parent-child relationships.

It's very satisfying for me when one of my mentees develops personally or professionally, and does well or achieves something remarkable. It gives my life meaning. I'm actually grateful to my mentees for giving me the opportunity to feel so purposeful. I know that sounds idealistic, and maybe it is. But it also happens to be true.

There's another way in which mentoring is a gift to us mentors. These young adults are part of our legacy that will live on long after we and our contemporaries are no longer here. This brings to mind Andrew Zenoff, the son of a friend of mine.

The Mentee Extraordinaire

Andrew was a child when we first met, but we really connected when he was 27. Shortly thereafter he sought my advice on business and life, and we've spoken regularly over the last decade and a half. We've become very close over the years, and our relationship has greatly added to my life:

> *Thanks to you, I realized that playing an active mentoring and coaching role with people I care about could be both enormously satisfying and personally enlightening. I have to give you credit for really starting that dimension of my life and honing those skills for me. I can now help other people*

and therefore feel more useful and purposeful. That was a big deal and represents an important part of my life today. I'm also gratified that you "paid it forward" by helping so many others.

Above the meaning, the learning, and the impact is the very special relationship that has evolved between us over the years. The support, joy, and love that I've received from you have been real and profound blessings in my life.

Faith Warriors

Many of you have been born into and raised in a certain belief system, but other people in your life may have helped you shape and distill your values as well. Perhaps you've had relationships with individuals who have allowed you to be less ego-driven, helped you look at life and death in the larger context, brought you peace, or showed you how to look at your fellow human beings differently. It's hard to get this on your own. That's a major gift.

I feel a presence of God in my life, but I haven't been religious in the formal sense of the word over the years. I do admire and appreciate the power faith plays in the lives of some of the people close to me, however. I'd like to introduce three of them to you now.

The Confidant

Steve Lyman and I meet regularly to process life's issues together. We refer to these conversations as "coffee dates" because they're frequent and meaningful and last an hour or so. The depth of our relationship is as if we've been lifelong friends:

> *Let me capture a few of the ways you've influenced my life. Your devotion to family and to your faith, along with the joyfulness that you bring to everything you do, serve as important reminders of those things to me. Your willingness to work on difficult issues speaks volumes about you and adds immeasurably to my life.*
>
> *You always set a really high standard when it comes to philanthropy. I'll never forget your generosity to the Elementary Institute of Science, a place near and dear to my heart. I'd be hard-pressed to think of anybody who has a larger heart as close to the surface as you. It's like a grand slam of generosity.*
>
> *I also love the fun component of you: your capacity to tell humorous stories. And nothing could ever replace the joy I get from our conversations about issues that are so central to who we are. Whether we are together or not, I feel your presence and support, and there is nothing that is more reassuring and comforting.*

The Family Man

Tom Ligouri is a fellow member of my San Diego forum. He's also the father of one of my mentees, Lisa. During our conversation, I'll never forget the moment he read a moving letter from Lisa about how our mentoring relationship had impacted her life. I loved that his daughter was comfortable sharing these thoughts with her dad, and that Tom was equally pleased to share the contents of the letter with me. As I told him:

> *Your reading this letter touches me on so many levels. One is that you're not only comfortable with my involvement with your daughter, but you're so appreciative of it, too. That says a lot about you as a man.*
>
> *I also marvel at your relationship with your own dad. When you told me years ago that you worked with your dad for 35 years <u>and</u> took a walk with him every day, that really struck me. It just typifies your "family first" focus, your personal discipline, your deeply held values, and your inner strength.*
>
> *I've been so impressed over the years by how you've been able to successfully cope with some of life's major disappointments by searching for the larger questions, as well as taking comfort in knowing that there is a plan for it all.*
>
> *What's equally remarkable is your loving and caring nature. You set the benchmark for showing up and being there, and it has enriched my life.*

The Helping Hand

Terry Meehan has been in the financial sector for most of his professional life, and after selling his company, he started an investment-advisory firm. He's also a very generous philanthropist and a man of deep faith.

On one occasion, Terry took a well-worn piece of paper from his wallet and gave it to me. It was his copy of "The Serenity Prayer," which he said he took comfort in by reading every day. I found the words to be quite poignant, but what moved me deeply was my friend's act of compassion in thinking that the prayer could help give me peace. This has inspired me in so many ways, as I told him:

> *I'm blessed to have your wisdom, kindness, and friendship in my life. Your spirituality, your keen insights into human behavior, and your philanthropic endeavors reflect the wisdom that's your essence.*
>
> *I know you practice your religion every day, but you don't lay it on anybody else. Still, you have this wonderful way of encouraging us to not take ourselves so seriously because there's something higher out there that's bigger than all of us. I like that. You've always been a guidepost, a barometer of spirituality for me.*
>
> *Your generosity and compassion are truly unmatched. You make it ordinary to do the extraordinary, whether it's in your support of Bread for*

*the World and other causes that you're passionate
about, or in your support of your good friends.*

*I wanted to let you know that these are indelible impressions that you've made on me, and that
I'm remarkably grateful to have you in my life.*

℗ ℗ ℗

The influence of the people on my journey cannot
be underestimated. I opened the window on some of
these relationships so you could feel the intensity of
my gratitude. However, please note that I chose these
individuals and these conversations because I felt they
might have the most relevance to *your* life and in no
way does this diminish the importance of those I have
not mentioned in this book.

I understand that you might not have, for example, business associates or mentees in your life, but you
may have a spouse and children. These are often the
closest relationships you'll ever have, and transcend
any of life's phases. So I've saved these very special
stories for last.

CHAPTER EIGHT

Across
the Years

*"Before someone's tomorrow has been
taken away, cherish those you love,
appreciate them today."*

— Michelle C. Ustaszeski

While my life seems to break down into distinct phases, and my life-changers tend to be grouped accordingly, there are three individuals who transcend all this: my wife and sons.

Over the years I've given my family many birthday, anniversary, Mother's Day, and other special-occasion cards. I've often shared handwritten messages with them. And I've had the opportunity to toast them at various celebrations. All of these have certainly been treasured times.

Like me, you might have captured memorable moments with your own family over the years. Yet we don't always think about expressing uncommon gratitude to our spouse and children, although they should be the most obvious choices. We may assume that they know how we feel. Or it might be the case that they're so close to us that we take them for granted, and we're not even aware of their contributions to our life until we stop and focus on them.

I'm so glad I took the time to focus on the most important people in *my* life.

The Family Team

My family is the cornerstone upon which my life has been built. In sharing my gratitude with my wife and sons, I expressed far more depth and breadth to them than anything I'd ever expressed before. In fact, these conversations were some of the richest and most emotional of my entire life. My family members said that the same was true for them, too.

So although the length of my conversations was similar for all of those on my victory lap, I thought it would be more instructive if I shared more of what I said to my immediate family members, since it's more likely that you have these types of relationships in your own life.

A Real Love Story:
My Conversation with My Wife, Lola

No matter how long you've been married, chances are your husband or wife is the most influential person in your life. If you've chosen to have kids together, your spouse is also the parent of your children. He or she helps create, nurture, and develop your sons and daughters, who will likely be your most important legacy. Getting married and having a family are major road-changers, setting you on a path that will last a lifetime.

I so looked forward to having my conversation with Lola. I wanted it to be in an unforgettable location, so I waited until we were together at a safari camp in Kenya. I'd expressed so much gratitude to her over the years in birthday and anniversary cards, on special occasions, and in the many private moments we'd had that I wasn't certain I'd be able to make this conversation one that was out of the ordinary. How wrong I was!

I began by asking myself one question: *How has my wife influenced my life?* I went on to write pages of notes to capture the many ways. Then, when it came time to share what I'd written, I could hardly hold back tears as I communicated these heartfelt emotions.

After recalling the most unusual way we met and the many memorable life experiences we've enjoyed together, this is what I expressed to my wife:

Lola, there is no one who's influenced my life more than you; not even close. Ever since I met you, you've either initiated or enthusiastically supported everything that has been important in my personal and professional life.

During our first five years of marriage, you moved with me four times to three different states; you gave birth to our twin sons; and you supported me in five different jobs, including the last one, a start-up business in a new industry that I invested our life savings in! And that was just the beginning. During the next 15 years, you carried the major responsibilities of parenthood, while I was consumed with building my company. No one could have been a more devoted and loving mother to our sons.

Over the years, you also set the standard for family celebrations, whether it was Thanksgiving holidays, surprise birthday parties, or get-togethers and reunions. To this day, people still talk about that unbelievable surprise weekend event for me that you spent nine months planning: bringing together my fraternity brothers for a 25-year reunion.

Your passion for travel—which took root when you lived in Europe during college and was beautifully expressed in the travel book you wrote, <u>Great Places by the Sea</u>—was another major influence in my life. Over the last two decades, we've visited so many places around the world that our "bucket list" is now mostly about revisiting.

In each house that I was able to buy, you made a warm and charming home for our family, no matter how limited our resources were at the time. Each one was filled with pictures of family and friends, tokens from the lifetime of deposits our memory bank has received.

Your love of people inspired you to focus on connecting us with so many interesting and special individuals no matter where we lived, and all I had to do was show up.

It wasn't just what you did, but how you did it. Your spontaneity and love of life have been an incredibly vital counterpoint to my structured and disciplined approach to almost everything I do.

I could have only dreamed that I'd meet someone whom I could love so fully—your eyes, your voice, your inner and outer beauty. It may sound trite, but my dream did come true. No 24-year-old could have made a better choice in marrying, and no man could have been more blessed.

Your enthusiastic support of my yearlong victory lap is an extraordinary gift. Most important, I'm forever grateful for your lifetime of profound love and devotion.

Sons and Daughters

Now, you may be thinking that your kids should be thanking *you,* especially after all you've given them.

You've sacrificed sleep, free time, personal pleasure, and so much more in order to provide for them, educate them, and care for them. They're the ones who should be grateful. Well, I couldn't agree with you more!

Yet whatever level of appreciation or gratitude your children have or have not expressed over the years doesn't preclude you from asking yourself this question: *Have my kids influenced my life in positive and significant ways?* If so, I encourage you to let them know in an out-of-the-ordinary way. I did, and it was the most important and poignant conversation I have ever had with each of my grown sons.

After I'd asked myself the question in the above paragraph, the answers flowed quite easily. Jonathan and Jason are fraternal twins, so I'd been their father for the exact same number of years. Nevertheless, I learned that the way each had influenced *me* was both special and unique.

Although I thought I'd expressed appreciation to them over the years, it was clear from how they responded that I'd never spoken to them in this way before. I also gave them whatever time they wanted to share what *I* had meant to *them*. It was evident from their reactions that what I'd hoped to model and articulate over the years had left a lasting impact, and my legacy was clear and reassuring. These two beautiful conversations alone would have made my yearlong journey worth the trip, and I'm so grateful that I didn't miss this opportunity.

I hope that sharing some of what I said to my sons may be a catalyst to stimulate your thinking about the impact your own sons or daughters have had on you, or at least give you a better understanding of the nature of these gratitude conversations.

ⓒ ⓒ ⓒ

The birth of my twin sons when I was 28 years old was a defining moment in my life. Virtually overnight, our family went from a dual-income couple with no children to a family of four with a single source of income. And to add to that anxiety-producing situation, the twins were only a year old when I chose to join a start-up business.

The early years were a constant struggle to provide both financially and emotionally for my family. Fortunately, Lola could understand the challenges we were facing and gave me critical support. But since our sons were too young to understand the circumstances at the time, my actions had to convey most of what I wanted them to learn. Being present was mandatory. Values were the focus.

During my conversation with my son Jonathan, he described the relationship between father and son as being like a "fine dance." He got it right; that perfectly describes the nature of our relationship, and I've felt that way from very early on.

Other than what I have with my wife, no relationship I've ever had has come anywhere close to the one

I've had with my boys. I always wanted them to have the best of me. That's when the dance began. I led.

Generations are different, of course, and times change. Even if my children were identical reproductions of me, they'd still have to dance to different music: their own. And although they're twins, my boys are very different from each other. So, over time, it's as if the music has changed and the moves have become more individually pronounced. That's why it is, in fact, a fine dance.

What remains the same for me are the values my sons and I share; along with the support, love, and respect we have for each other. This all makes up the stable and permanent dance floor of life. For me, being present is still mandatory. The difference now is that it's their move, and if I'm blessed, they'll reach out to me when they need me.

I'm deeply grateful for what I've learned from my sons, and I'd like to share a little of that with you now. First up is my oldest son, a title Jonathan earned by arriving five minutes before his brother.

Sports as a Metaphor for Life: My Conversation with My Son Jonathan

The golf resort I chose as the venue for our conversation truly "set the table" for our special time together. Jonathan and I could both celebrate the good fortune that had enabled us to enjoy the magnificent environment and special services the place offered. This is what I expressed to him:

During those early years when I was start-ing up my business, I'd rush home to put you to sleep and then continue to work into the night. I loved those special moments with you. It was a daily reminder that I had both a financial and psychological responsibility to you and the rest of our family. This was life's real deal, and I felt that I had this one chance to do it well.

As the years flew by, we made time to travel as a family and learned about other countries and their cultures. What a thrill it was to share these experiences with you.

Even more important, sports became part of our lives and have remained so to this day. We didn't just play touch football, Ping-Pong, tennis, and bas-ketball for fun when you were growing up; they were a vehicle for teaching teamwork, sportsmanship, competition, and many other life values.

When your interest in bodybuilding led to your designing and equipping the state-of-the-art fitness facility at our conference center when you were only 16 years old, this first time working together was very special for me.

I was also impressed by the major events you put on for disadvantaged kids while you were in college. I'll never forget what you did with the money you'd received as graduation gifts: In honor of your grandfathers, you donated the funds to be used at an "adopt a horse" program for handicapped kids. You said it was because your mother's dad was a doctor, and my father (whom you never knew) was someone who loved horses. To this day, I still get choked up when I think about it.

After graduation, your entrepreneurial instincts led you to a variety of start-up business opportunities. You were a trailblazer and always a decade or so ahead of the pack, whether it was your health-and-beauty magazine, your investment newsletter, or your Internet company.

From the time you were very young, you created special moments that have become major deposits in my memory bank. Many of them look like sports activities but are in fact so much more. Our father/son golf outings, or our frequent calls discussing games on television are all about connecting and sharing life. The sporting event just sets the table for a wide range of communication between us, going as deep as we wish at that moment.

I'll always remember when you took me to my first NBA game, which was so exciting that we've done it a few times since. And it's never just about the game; it's about the shared experiences, along with the wit and enthusiasm that you bring to these events.

I appreciate your unique way of doing things and the way you live your life, which has also influenced my behavior. You've helped me be more spontaneous—more flexible, light, and in the moment—which has enriched my life and my love for you. What more could I ask for.

It's no surprise to me that immediately following our victory-lap conversation, Jonathan and I played golf on one of our favorite courses. And there's no one with whom I'd rather share a round.

Touching All the Bases:
My Conversation with My Son Jason

I had my conversation with Jason in Kenya. We'd just heard the Kenyan Boys Choir perform at dinner, and we returned to the peace and quiet of our room to talk. We started with the usual trip down memory lane, and then I shared the following with him:

I have to note the added excitement I feel having our conversation take place while we're on a Free The Children mission. It's hard to describe the joyfulness and gratitude I feel that you were able to take nine days away from your family, your business, and your other obligations to join me on this journey.

As we have reflected on the highlights of our life together, it's very gratifying to observe that family celebrations, travel experiences, and sports were important parts of your development. What was equally important was your focus on education and relevant work experience during high school, college, Harvard Business School, and thereafter, which ultimately led to your becoming a founder and general partner of your own venture-capital firm. Somehow, you also made time to assume leadership positions in the nonprofit arena.

In your personal life, you were equally deliberate and discriminating in the choice of your good friends and in Ann, your beautiful and intelligent wife. Of course, your mother's life and my own have also been changed and forever enriched by the birth of Claire and Wilson, who are sources of great pride and joy for us. I'll never forget the warmth and deep emotion I feel when they jump on our bed to wake us up when we're visiting you.

I've told you over the years how proud I am of these achievements, and they are indeed significant. You have, without a doubt, touched all the bases. But it's more than your accomplishments I want to acknowledge; it's how you've done things so far in your life. You approach each and every educational experience, travel activity, work assignment, or family affair in a thoughtful and purposeful way; and always with integrity and excellence.

There's something else I've wanted to highlight, which has left a profound impact on me. As you know, I've received most of my meaning in life from helping others, especially those who are important to me. Nothing is more gratifying than helping my family, along with those people and organizations who are highly valued by them. On several occasions you've reached out to me to be helpful to individuals or causes that were important to you.

The first such occasion I remember was when you asked me to help you launch a forum-like support group for you and your friends. How thrilling that was for me. Over the years, you've also suggested to your friends that they reach out to me so that I could help them get clarity in their lives or deal with a life issue, and I loved being helpful to them. Another event that was a big deal for me was when you asked me to facilitate a critical strategy meeting with a charitable organization you supported.

It's certainly satisfying when one's grown son seeks out his father's advice and counsel, but it's beyond satisfying to be engaged in helping both friends of yours and causes that mean a lot to you.

When I finished my tribute to Jason, he surprised me with his own. My son read the following poem he'd written for me, words that will be eternally emblazoned upon my heart:

> *You gave me life*
> *You gave me love*
> *You gave me a huge head start*
> *And you got out of the way.*
> *For that I am forever grateful.*

Later, he also inscribed the words in a 60-page album of more than 100 pictures, stories, and maps that he compiled and presented to me as a reminder of the extraordinary time we spent together in Kenya.

    ⊛ ⊛ ⊛

In his book *Creating the Good Life,* James O'Toole noted: "Aristotle says our most important and rewarding human capacity is to learn new ideas and, especially, to apply that learning to helping and teaching others."

I'm hopeful that what you've read so far has indeed been instructive for you. And I'm confident that the next part of the book will provide you with everything you need to start putting together your own expressions of gratitude.

    ⊛ ⊛ ⊛ ⊛ ⊛

PART III

YOUR
MOMENT

CHAPTER NINE

Do It
Your Way

*"To speak gratitude is courteous and pleasant,
to enact gratitude is generous and noble,
but to live gratitude is to touch heaven."*

— JOHANNES A. GAERTNER

If I have convinced you to experience the pleasure of expressing heartfelt gratitude, I'm confident that you'll ultimately figure out how to do so. Once you know that it's the right thing to do, you don't need to get too caught up in the mechanics of it. That said, I would like to offer some suggestions to help you get started.

When you start to plan your own tributes, you still might have to refocus your thinking with respect to the ways we usually convey appreciation in our society. As I mentioned earlier in the book, while we frequently tell each other "Thanks," *truly* thanking someone in a way that isn't so casual is just not typically done.

The distinction is this: It's not just about appreciating who these people *are;* it's about expressing uncommon gratitude for *what they've done for you and what they've meant to your life*. Put another way, how is your life different because these individuals were in it?

For those of you who are motivated to take action, it's as easy as answering these four questions:

1. *Who could I do this with?*
2. *What do I communicate to them?*
3. *Where and how could I deliver the message?*
4. *How could I follow up?*

Let's tackle them one at a time.

1. Who Could I Do This With?

First, you're going to make your list. The number of names on it is inconsequential; what's crucial is that each person you list has had a profound, long-term effect on your life. Whether that influence is the result of some ongoing action or was a onetime event, it's the depth of the impact that's important.

If thinking about the kinds of people who have influenced you in this way is difficult, here is a partial list to help you get started:

- *Family member:* parent, grandparent, brother, sister, son, daughter, spouse, life partner, aunt, uncle, cousin, in-law.

- *Teacher:* sports coach, mentor, guidance counselor, professor, life coach, lecturer, seminar leader, colleague.

- *Health provider:* doctor, dentist, psychologist, physical therapist, chiropractor, fitness trainer.

- *Professional:* employer, partner, boss, co-worker, investor, banker, consultant.

- *Personal advisor:* lawyer, tax preparer, financial or investment advisor, insurance broker, real-estate agent.

- *Friend:* lifelong or close confidant, neighbor.

- *Life enhancer:* artist, musician, writer, interior designer, architect.

- *Spiritual leader:* priest, minister, rabbi.

- *Public servant:* police officer, firefighter, EMT, political representative.

- *Service provider:* caregiver, home helper, housekeeper, hairstylist.

- *Student:* mentee, apprentice, subordinate.

- *Member(s) of an affiliate group:* Boy or Girl Scout, fraternity brother or sorority sister, sports teammate, workout buddy, fellow hobbyist, book-club member, religious congregant.

Now that you've identified the men and women who have been meaningful in your life, you may want to reflect on how they've impacted you. Maybe they have:

- Instilled values and principles

- Added meaning to your life

- Influenced your career path

- Introduced you to other important relationships

- Taught you skills

- Provided an inspiring example with their actions or reactions to challenges

- Been there through thick and thin

- Contributed to the quality of your life

- Provided you with excellent professional service

- Introduced joy, pleasure, and laughter into your world

- Literally saved your life

There are other ways in which you can approach the making of your list. You could break your life down into phases or decades, and think about who the road-changers were during each particular era of your life. For example, you might have been greatly affected by someone who helped take care of you in childhood. As a young married parent, perhaps you had an older neighbor who was always there with advice and support when you needed it. If you're retired, maybe someone introduced you to a new activity or hobby that reinvigorated you or reignited your passion.

The times we live in now may have brought a whole new category of life-changer into your life. If you've been laid off, lost your home, or seen your retirement savings dwindle, there could be professional advisors or people working in various agencies and organizations—or even friends or family—who have shepherded you through these tough times or helped guide your life in new directions.

In fact, you might find that these trying times are actually creating many opportunities to express deep gratitude, which will be especially appreciated now. The challenges you're facing could even be the catalyst for making you more aware of the power of extraordinary gratitude.

2. What Do I Communicate to Them?

When you've made your list, you'll want to frame your expressions of gratitude by reflecting on exactly what it is that makes you so appreciative of each person. Be explicit, not only about his or her contribution to your life but the specifics of that impact as well. The more precise and exact you can be, the more likely it is that the individual you're talking to will fully appreciate your gratitude.

Some things to consider are:

- Was it a singular act, several situations, or a lifetime of influence or role-modeling that impacted you?

- Where did it take place? Setting the stage can add meaning.

- What was it about that moment (or series of events) that made it so life-changing for you?

- What did it feel like then, and why is it still so important to you?

I recommend writing down just how each person impacted your life. You can be brief. To get you thinking, here are some examples of the kinds of things you might be expressing appreciation and gratitude for, followed by how you can be more specific and dig even deeper:

- "Your character and solid values have been great role models for me."

  Specifically: "I was impressed seeing you cope so gracefully with the disappointment of losing your job and having to make lifestyle changes."

  Digging Deeper: "This brought home what's important in my life, and I made some important adjustments myself."

- "You're the very definition of a 'good man/woman.'"

  Specifically: "Hanging in there through the ups and downs of your marriage, and then taking in your aging mother-in-law, showed me what decent behavior really is."

  Digging Deeper: "You've made me rethink my relationships with important people in my own life."

- "You provide me with stability and comfort."

  Specifically: "No matter how stressful things get at work, I always know that I'm going to come home to a serene environment and your unfailing support."

Digging Deeper: "This makes me want to do the same for you, and I think I'm a better person for it."

- "You opened doors for me that have led to career opportunities."

Specifically: "Without that introduction to your uncle Edward and the good word you put in for me, I never would have gotten started in this field."

Digging Deeper: "I love what I do, and you've been instrumental in my feeling happy and fulfilled. It makes me want to help others when I can."

- "You were always my champion."

Specifically: "That time you stood up for me when I let the department down prevented me from getting fired."

Digging Deeper: "Your trust in me spurred me to up my game, and I believe that I'm a better employee and colleague for it. Plus, I have learned what it means to be supportive of others."

- "You 'get' me."

  Specifically: "You were the only one who wasn't horrified when I quit my job and opened a cheese shop/moved to Tibet/ devoted my life to tattooing/whatever."

  Digging Deeper: "Your acceptance allows me the freedom to be myself when I'm around you, and that's a great gift. Through your example, I find that I'm less judgmental of other people."

- "You're a rock."

  Specifically: "It's a relief for me to know that there's someone I can trust with the most confidential aspects of my life."

  Digging Deeper: "You epitomize loyalty, and that gives me tremendous peace of mind. It makes me want to be there for the people who rely on me."

- "You're my most reliable sounding board."

  Specifically: "You were so patient when I was trying to decide which home to buy, and your clearheaded thinking helped me make the right decision."

Digging Deeper: "It reminded me how helpful another person can be, even when it comes to significant personal decisions."

- "You make me laugh and always lighten the moment."

  Specifically: "Every time I think about that road trip we took and how we laughed from coast to coast, I get enjoyment from it all over again."

  Digging Deeper: "I learned how humor can help me stay in the present moment, as well as how to enjoy life more fully."

Don't be surprised if the person is deeply touched by the fact that something he or she did had such a long-lasting impact on you.

3. Where and How Could I Deliver the Message?

Now that you know whom you want to express gratitude to and why you're so appreciative of them, it's time to decide how best to deliver your message.

I believe that making the effort to have a face-to-face meeting brings a sense of true importance to the occasion. But in order for this process to be pleasurable as well as meaningful, it's essential that you choose the form of delivery that's most comfortable.

In other words, having the conversation in person might not be right for you if you feel that you're unable to freely express your emotions verbally; or if you are concerned that you don't have the language skills to do it, are generally reserved, or get embarrassed easily. Also, don't just think about what suits *you* best; keep in mind what would be most meaningful to, and comfortable for, the person receiving your message.

Meet

If you do decide to meet in person, choosing the ideal place to have your conversation can enhance the experience. You'll want it to be:

- *Quiet.* You'll need a place where you can talk comfortably and be in a distraction-free environment. I found that either homes or secluded open spaces worked best. Although one of the most common places people get together to talk is over a meal in a restaurant, I don't recommend this. Not only can it be too noisy to talk or to record your conversation (if you decide to do so), but you'll also be constantly interrupted by the waitstaff and other things going on around you.

- *At a specifically designated time.* It's ideal if the conversation can be independent of any other activity, but that's not always possible or practical. If you do elect to deliver your gratitude message in conjunction with a vacation; during a road trip; before or after a family, college, or high-school reunion; at a conference; or based around some other event, see if you can set aside a time and place separate from the other activities to have your conversation.

- *Meaningful to the other person (or both of you).* I discovered that quite often the setting added to the special nature of the occasion. It might be nice to have your conversation where you first met, in a place you've spent time together in the past, or somewhere new that you know he or she will appreciate.

- *Somewhere you could prolong the moment.* I think it's nice to plan to follow your conversation with some pursuit that you and the other person both enjoy.

If no occasion to meet in person presents itself, or the distance between you is so great that having a meeting is difficult or impossible to arrange, you can find other ways in which to express your gratitude.

Write

Can writing a letter be a powerful vehicle to convey profound gratitude? Absolutely. A study at Kent State University focused on students who wrote to the people who had impacted their lives. The instruction the students received about the letters was that they should be positively expressive, offer some insight and reflection, not be trivial, and convey a high level of appreciation or gratitude.

Over a six-week period, the students reported that their feelings of happiness and satisfaction increased considerably. Furthermore, 75 percent of the people in the study said that they planned to maintain their new gratitude habits when the study concluded. This study was just about the givers, not the receivers. But given what I know now, I think I can safely surmise that the recipients of the letters were equally happy and satisfied.

If you're thinking about this option, note that e-mail is fine, but a handwritten letter is particularly special these days.

Call

You can certainly make your expression of gratitude in a phone call. However, if you opt to do it this way, I'd suggest making an appointment to talk rather than calling casually. This conveys the message that what you have to say is important. You also want to make sure the person is available for the amount of time you need.

Be Creative

You might come up with your own way of delivering your gratitude message that I never would have thought of, perhaps courtesy of the numerous technological opportunities available today. You could have a "face-to-face" meeting via webcam, or record what you have to say on a CD or DVD and send that to the people on your list. If you're skilled, you could add music or other production values.

I'll bet that many of you have talents you can call on for this process. Could you write a story or a song? This brings to mind a woman I met at a conference not long ago. As we talked about this very topic, she told me that she had a talent for calligraphy. She said that she'd once written a letter in beautiful script to a former teacher and had received a wonderful response to it. By the time we'd finished talking, she was thinking about doing a letter a month to others in her life. Isn't that a great idea?

I heard another great idea recently while at a dinner party. As I talked to a man who was visiting from Minnesota, my gratitude journey came up. This man told me that four years ago, he and his three siblings had hired a writer of personal poems to create one for their mother's 75th birthday. The poet interviewed each of the adult children and then wrote the poem based on what they'd told her about their mother. That poem was then read to their mother at her birthday celebration, and she was deeply touched by it. I told my new friend that I thought this was a wonderful act of extraordinary gratitude.

But that's not the end of the story. Unbeknownst to her children at the time, the mother went on to write a letter of appreciation to the poet, saying how important that poem was to her. She told the poet that she was profoundly touched by the message because she was uncertain that she'd been a good mother, and this poem had put her mind at rest. The mother apparently was unable to share this self-doubt with her own adult children, so when she died four years later, the poet decided to share the letter with the family.

The man at the dinner party and his siblings would never have known the impact the poem had had on their mother had she not written this letter. And how sad if the mother had died without ever receiving the gratitude expressed in that poem.

The most important thing is that whatever you do must meet the definition of being an *extraordinary and uncommon* way to express gratitude.

4. How Could I Follow Up?

Although I made a memento for each of the people on my journey, you don't need to do anything elaborate or go to a lot of expense to create a memorable keepsake. You could take the idea of any one of the components I had in mine: a framed photo, a CD of the conversation, or a handwritten note.

On the other hand, some of you will have the skills to take what I did and make a more sophisticated presentation. Still others will have interests that lend themselves to coming up with different types of mementos, perhaps a collage, a scrapbook, or a photo album.

If you don't feel that you could create something yourself, there are many companies that specialize in crafting personalized gifts. For example, Oprah Winfrey commissioned a quilt honoring the life and work of Maya Angelou, her friend and mentor, and presented it to her on her birthday a few years ago. A little online research will yield ideas in your particular fields of interest and that are within your budget.

The idea behind this memento is that it acknowledges that what you've shared with this person is significant enough to commemorate. By sending a keepsake, you're sharing the sense of importance you have about your expression of gratitude with each of the people you've chosen to do this with.

Giving the individuals on your list something that can be displayed in some manner rather than just being stuck in a drawer means that it can be enjoyed and shared with their own loved ones. For this reason, I like the idea of framing or recording something because it lends even more meaning and permanence to the memento and speaks to how special the recipient is to the giver.

Finally, a memento that has longevity gives the recipient the opportunity to enjoy the memory of the experience. Remember that framed note and picture my 11-year-old son made for his mother? Many years later, it's still displayed on the wall in her office.

❦ ❦ ❦

I'm most hopeful that by now I've raised your awareness of the universal value of expressing gratitude, and you'll find your own uncommon way to do so with someone who has made a real difference in your life. Many people whom I've shared my story with have already gone on their own gratitude journeys, and I'm hopeful that nothing will stand in *your* way as you prepare to do the same.

❦ ❦ ❦ ❦ ❦

CHAPTER TEN

HESITANCY IS JUST
ONE STEP FROM ACTION

"Appreciation can make a day, even change a life.
Your willingness to put it into words
is all that is necessary."

— MARGARET COUSINS

This chapter is a call to action. Here's the question: if someone who was important to you died abruptly, would you say to yourself, "I wish I would have . . ."? Or what about this: if something were to happen to you suddenly, wouldn't you want those you care about to have known how much you appreciated them? That's the core issue here, so really stop and think about it. If your answer to the questions I've posed is yes, then expressing your deep gratitude will make sense to you and could become much easier to do.

That said, I'm afraid that there will be some of you who have read this far and, although you grasp the concept and think it's a great idea, will still not act. You know about the pleasure, the peace of mind, and the deepening of relationships that can be gained from doing this, as well as the pain of regret that's almost certain if you don't. Some of you may have actually experienced this pain already.

You know how meaningful it will be to the recipient of your gratitude, and there is no downside to the process. So what could possibly be keeping you from moving forward? What are the obstacles?

In this chapter, I'll explore some of the rationalizations that might cause you to avoid embarking on this journey. I'm going to address each of them, one by one, in the hopes that I might help you overcome your apprehension.

"I'm Too Young"

The implication here is that you can't think of anyone who has profoundly impacted your life as yet. But that isn't true, as even young people can come up with *someone:* maybe a parent, grandparent, teacher, or coach. I know if you really give this some thought, you'll be able to think of a few names.

There are several good reasons to start expressing your appreciation to these people *now.* The sooner you tell them how you feel, the longer they will be able to take pleasure in the message. Why wait until they're old or dying? If they do die, there's no chance at all that they will ever fully appreciate your level of gratitude. How much better would it be for them to know the impact they made upon you for whatever years they have left? They'll probably be inspired to help others; in fact, the ripples may very well be felt far and wide, and all because you made these individuals aware of how important they are to you.

Also, keep in mind that expressing your gratitude will likely enhance and enrich your relationships with these wonderful human beings, and by starting young, you'll have more time to enjoy them.

Another consideration is that it's often easier for a young person to speak openly and express heartfelt feelings. Plus, the earlier you do so, the more likely it is that you'll get better at it, and the effort will become habitual. Once again, it's like exercising an undeveloped muscle.

Finally, these expressions of gratitude can be defining moments in your own life, and it's never too soon to start having those. *This is the moment!*

"I'm Too Old"

When it comes to "I'm too old," I believe what you're really thinking is that many of the individuals who impacted your life are already gone. I'll bet there are some of you who are old enough to have attended many funerals and have thought, *I wish I had told David how I felt about him.* And yet you don't tell *Diane,* who is still alive, how important she is to you.

While it's true that some of the most influential people—or the easiest to identify as such—often show up in our lives when we're younger, there are road-changers at all stages of life. Rarely are any of us so old that there isn't a single person in our lives who would be deeply touched to be recognized in a special way.

I'm also aware that older men and women are not in the habit of openly expressing feelings, and there are few role models for doing so at this time. Although it may be true that women find it easier to emote, I hope that this book has demonstrated that an "older guy" can do it, too.

Do keep in mind that there is one big advantage older people have in this process: they have a lifetime of gratitude they can express to those who have really mattered, as well as the wisdom to know what is truly important at the end of the day.

"I Don't Know That Many People"

Do you feel left out of this process because you don't have anywhere near 44 names on your list? Well, don't worry—many people probably feel the way you do. There may be just a couple of individuals you'd like to acknowledge, while others will have more. Whatever the case, I can assure you that we all know someone who's impacted us.

In any event, it's not the *number* of men and women on your list that's important; it's the depth of the impact they've made. I know some people who have started with one name, and the personal gratification was so great that they've now added more. As my friend Charlie told me, he's never instigated something that has turned into "pure gold" quite like expressing deep gratitude.

"I Can't Afford It"

I recognize that it's highly unlikely that anyone will take a journey similar to my yearlong victory lap. I was fortunate to have the time and resources to devote to this significant undertaking, and it was also important for me to do it in this way.

All of our life circumstances are different, however, and our processes and journeys will of course go in various directions. I did things *my* way, and you should do them *your* way. For example, you don't have to travel around the country having face-to-face conversations with people. If you do want to meet in person, you can start with those close to home and schedule others during vacations, holiday visits, business trips, and so forth.

Writing a letter costs the paper it's written on and a stamp, and e-mails and phone calls are virtually free. In other words, everyone can afford to make these expressions of gratitude. The investment is low and the payoff is high, and there are so few opportunities in life that this can be said for. How you go about conveying your messages is entirely up to you; just design a way that's meaningful but doable (and affordable) for you.

"It Doesn't Really Matter"

Someone recently told me, "I just don't feel that what I'd say to somebody would make that much of a difference to him or her." I'm no psychologist, but I have had lots of interactions with other people over the years, and I'm of the opinion that most don't give themselves enough credit for who they are and what they mean to others. Your words and your actions *do* mean a lot to many. I'm confident of that. See what happens when you take the time to express how much someone means to you. After doing so, I highly doubt that anyone is going to feel, *Well, it doesn't really matter.*

Further, from my experience, I can tell you that expressing your gratitude to another will be important to *you,* too. If you're still not convinced, give it a try just once—the outcome may surprise you.

"I'd Be Uncomfortable"

The first time doing anything can be challenging, much like when you first got on a bicycle or learned how to swim. Once you tried it a few times, though, I'll bet it became hard to remember what it was like to be apprehensive.

It's understandable that the thought of your first conversation may make you feel uncomfortable or give you a little performance anxiety. Yet in my experience, this feeling disappears far faster than the time it takes to learn how to ride a bike or swim. I do understand that, just as with any new habit, the first time is the most difficult.

Remember, I didn't just sit down and have these conversations off the cuff; rather, I took the time to specifically think about what I'd like to say. As soon as I thought about the person and jotted down what I was grateful for, the words came easily. I took the notes with me, which I thought might be awkward but wasn't. Referring to my notes periodically during the conversation reminded me that I wouldn't leave out any important points, and this helped me relax.

Having said all that, I think it might be easier if you can see what another person would say on his or her own gratitude journey. That's why I've put so many of my own expressions of appreciation in this book. You can see how some of them might relate to people in *your* life and use them as a starting point for formulating your own heartfelt tributes.

"*They'd* Be Uncomfortable"

People like to receive things in different ways. In his book *The Five Love Languages,* Gary Chapman presents some relevant ideas. He says that we all like to give and receive love in five broad categories of expression: words of affirmation, quality time, receiving gifts, acts of service, and physical touch. I'm not saying that you need to follow any particular method for expressing or receiving gratitude. What I'm suggesting is that you should look for the best way for *you,* as well as the one that would be most comfortable for the person receiving it, based on your knowledge of who he or she is.

I must admit that the idea of a personal meeting created a little anxiety among a few of the people I invited to participate in my victory lap. Some weren't exactly sure what the conversation would be about, even after I gave them the outline. But I knew these individuals very well and felt confident that I'd be able to make them comfortable with the process. You'll have to make your own assessment about how to go about this, although you do have one advantage I didn't have. You can ask the person if he or she is familiar with the book *This Is the Moment!*

"I'm Self-Made"

If you take pride in feeling self-made, paying tribute to those who have made a real difference in your life can feel at odds with this perception of yourself. Expressing profound gratitude may seem as if you're diminishing your own achievements; after all, how could you have all this assistance and support and still be self-made?

I do think this position has merit. Being successful absolutely requires hard work, persistence, creativity, and so much more (including luck). But upon closer inspection, I don't think anyone is, in fact, self-made. Without parents, colleagues, family, or friends, where would any of us be? Nowhere. And that's the point. We've *all* had support and guidance from many along the way.

"Everyone Already Knows How I Feel"

For the most part, I think that our words and actions over the years probably do convey how we feel about other people. That's a great first step, but it likely leaves a lot unsaid, and you know by now the unfortunate consequences of leaving things unsaid.

It's become clear to me that all of the men and women on my victory lap knew how I felt about them before I took my journey. What they could not fully appreciate, because I had never adequately expressed it, was the depth and full dimension of my gratitude for what they'd meant to me. And before I took the time to reflect on these contributions, I wasn't even fully aware myself.

"I Don't Know Where They Are"

According to government statistics, more than 40 million Americans relocate every year. It's no wonder that it's so easy to lose track of people, even when they've been important to us at an earlier stage of our lives. Time and distance often intervene to break our connections, and I'm not immune from this myself. There were a couple of fellows from my early years in business whom I would have liked to have had on my own list, but I was unable to locate them.

When planning my gratitude journey, I began to realize that I'm an aficionado of rich, lifelong relationships. Some of my friends collect wine, while others are really into art or cars. Not me. I get pleasure and satisfaction from staying in touch with and nurturing those relationships, and that's one reason why there were so many people on my list.

I hadn't kept up with everyone, of course. I mentioned earlier that several years ago, my wife surprised me with a 25-year reunion of my fraternity brothers from the University of Michigan (and their spouses!), most of whom I hadn't seen since we left college. Lola tracked them down all over the country without ever having met any of them before, and this was in the days before there were Internet resources for reconnecting with lost friends.

Now, with so many options available on "friend finding" Websites and social networking, it's easier than ever to find even long-lost pals and colleagues. The process of looking for them can be a lot of fun, and reconnecting with them is usually very satisfying.

"I'm Too Busy"

We all know that feeling when good intentions come up against the multitude of demands in our lives. It happens all too often that new objectives get deferred or, worse yet, never get done. Having said that, I'm encouraged by the fact that you've read this far. I believe that if I've successfully demonstrated the importance of expressing gratitude, you'll make time for it. The good news is that this actually takes very little time to do. Expressing profound gratitude in an uncommon way can be life-changing, but it doesn't require you to make significant changes in your life.

In the next chapter, you're going to read about a friend of mine who took 15 minutes to write a letter that gave him closure on a relationship going back more than 50 years! It's rare to find something so fulfilling and significant that can take less than an hour to do, and do well. So however you organize your day, try making expressing gratitude "number one" on your to-do list just once. I think you'll be happy you did.

"<u>They're</u> Too Busy"

This might be the response you'll get from people on your list if they believe that the visit is for their benefit alone. They may just not place a high enough priority on it, meaning that it will never get done. However, if they know it's important to *you,* it's more likely that they'll make your conversation a higher priority. So make that point: ask them to do this for you.

Yet even if you do so, it may be that your friends' lives are just too frenetic, and they simply can't set aside a few hours for you. Rather than using that as a reason for not delivering your message at all, think of doing it in another way.

I found myself in that exact same situation when trying to connect with Craig Kielburger of Free The Children. I called Craig to arrange a visit with him so that I could convey my profound appreciation to him, but he and his colleagues happened to be in Haiti at the time.

Free The Children has built nine schools, a nutrition center, and sanitation facilities in Haiti; and they've helped support teacher salaries and technical training for students there. So they were in the perfect position to provide help and resources during the aftermath of the catastrophic earthquake that hit the island in early 2010.

I don't doubt that Craig will soon be off somewhere else when the need arises, so it would have been very easy for me to think: *He's too busy; I'll get to it sometime or other.*

But then my inner voice spoke to me, asking, *Who knows what could happen to either of us in the meantime?* Reminding myself that *this is the moment,* I'd like to take this opportunity to express my gratitude to Craig right here, and right now:

> *Dear Craig,*
>
> *I met you when you were still a teenager. You approached me at a reception and asked me to tell you about a project that you knew was dear to me, the Elementary Institute of Science. I said I'd be happy to do so if you'd first tell me why a teenager would care.*

I was amazed by your story—how you read a newspaper article at age 12 about child slave labor and made a decision to found Free The Children to do what you could to stop it. I've never been the same after that conversation. I'll always remember thinking, <u>If this teenager can help kids in developing countries while enlightening young people in Canada and the United States, how could I not dream big and do my share?</u>

We stayed in touch, and then you called and asked if I'd facilitate the launching of your book <u>Me to We: Finding Meaning in a Material World.</u> Facetiously, I said that I'd be the perfect person to help since I had no experience whatsoever in the launching of a book. I wasn't deterred by the fact that you were really well known in Canada but much less so in the United States. I'll never forget how you related to the audiences I arranged, from the very young and under-served to the older and privileged. I'd be remiss if I didn't tell you how exciting and gratifying it was to me when you told me that your book had made the bestsellers list.

In 2008 I visited the Free The Children headquarters in Toronto, the hub of your organization that now employs some 120 individuals in North America and 50 in other countries. The week of my visit, you and your people put on a motivational day for 8,000 young people in Toronto, which was also telecast to many more thousands of students in schools throughout Canada. It was a spectacularly inspiring occasion that I'll never forget.

And then, last but not least, my participation with my son on a Free The Children mission to Kenya in August 2009 was life-changing and has magnified the fulfillment of my life.

It's natural for me to think about the take-home value of everything I'm a part of, from business meetings to life experiences. To that end, I'm reminded daily of that mission to Kenya, and the impressions it made on me will last a lifetime. The ready access of electric power, drinking water, food, technology, and the comforts of home that I enjoy every day all have increased appreciation for me now.

I've seen firsthand how you and this organization are not only saving lives in developing countries, but are enriching the lives of countless young men and women from Canada and the United States who embark on these missions with you and your people.

My participation in these initiatives has provided another dimension of meaning and purpose in my life and will do so in the future as well: my son has become involved in supporting the efforts of Free The Children, and so have some of his friends.

I wish I'd had the chance to share these feelings with you in person. I'm hopeful we'll have that opportunity to do so sometime in the future.

*In the meantime, I won't have to regret the fact
that I was unable to convey the profound impact
you have had on my life. The fact that you are 28
years of age makes it all the more remarkable.*

*With much affection and respect,
Walter*

I hadn't even finished all of the conversations on
my victory lap when I started to get feedback from
several people who had chosen to embark upon this
journey themselves. And it wasn't just those who
were participants in *my* victory lap; it was friends of
friends, and those I didn't even know. It seems like
this was an idea whose time had come, but, in reality,
it was long overdue.

CHAPTER ELEVEN

IGNITING SPARKS

*"How wonderful it is that nobody
need wait a single moment before
starting to improve the world."*

— ANNE FRANK

In retrospect, I now realize that not only was I giving a gift of gratitude to people very important to me, I was also awakening the recipients to the idea of doing the same thing with others. This has magnified my original gift greatly.

It is my hope that my victory lap will become a springboard for countless individuals such as you to pay gratitude forward. My dream is that I will be the one to get this concept launched, but that there will then be enough remarkable men and women to keep it going. It seems that others are indeed getting the message, and it's already happening in ways I couldn't have imagined at the outset. I'd like to think that what Andrew Zenoff so articulately said to me is true: "Your victory lap is a wildfire of love and gratitude, and sparks are igniting everywhere."

The first "sparks" that came back to me were courtesy of my own family members. My son Jason was motivated to call an old high-school friend who helped inspire his passion for computers, which has become an important component in his personal life and career. Although they hadn't actually spoken since graduation, Jason's expression of gratitude rekindled the relationship.

Then I heard from my nephew, Eric Herrenkohl (his mother, Ellen, is Lola's sister, and one of my 44 as well). Eric has his own one-man firm in the field of organizational and personal development, and I've mentored him for several years. He's very smart and immediately understood what I'd been doing.

"As soon as you told me about your victory lap, and then when I experienced for myself how encouraging and meaningful it was for me, it clicked," he said. "I realized that I could turn a potential negative—regretting that I'd never told the most important people in my life how much they mean to me and why—into a huge win. Something positive—carving out the time to be with them and communicate with them—would be the end result."

Eric set up a time to have his own gratitude conversation with his parents. "Interestingly, a number of things I said were surprising to them," he told me. "As you know, these are pretty intuitive people. But parents do and say so many things that have an impact on their kids, despite the fact that they don't seem to be getting through at the time. I wouldn't have had this conversation if you hadn't taken the initiative to have a session with me, so thank you."

This story of how my nephew captured the moment with his parents is both beautiful and remarkable. But for me, it's also a vivid and wonderful example of how we can pay it forward.

The Gift That Keeps on Giving

Soon I was hearing from others on my list, too. The always-impressive Doris Anderson of the Elementary Institute of Science (EIS) seized the moment by telling me: "Your victory lap turned out to be a teachable moment for young people that character matters, and in identifying some of the things that are really important in life.

"On your victory lap, you looked back and noted the character traits in a person that honor your relationship," she continued. "At EIS, we focus on the character traits of students that will establish them as well-respected citizens both now and in their future. Therefore, we've established a 'character matters' program, along with a character-education coordinator who will help the students hone the skills of character development. This was all due to your victory lap, which made us see the importance of recognizing good character! When young people have shared values such as honoring relationships, they begin to see what a better place this planet could be."

Michael Mack, a member of my San Diego forum (and the current moderator), was originally skeptical about the idea and stated plainly that he was uncertain of its value. He did, however, agree to participate for my sake. So it was both surprising and rewarding to hear from him about a high-school reunion he attended shortly after our conversation.

"During the course of the weekend I, along with other members of the football team, had the chance to meet with our coach and take some pictures," he said. "I turned to him at the close of our photo session and told him that after my father, he had been one of the most influential men in my life, both as a mentor and role model. I described the attributes I admired in this man and how they had influenced me, and then I thanked him. The coach immediately teared up and turned away, both embarrassed to be crying and touched by my words. I felt that an important step in both of our lives had occurred."

Another who took action was Steve Lyman, who told me that he'd contacted several old friends and rekindled some very significant relationships: "One reconnection was with a former business associate whom I hadn't spoken to, except through Christmas cards, in 15 years. How sad is that? Time absolutely flew by, and tears were rolling down both of our cheeks as we recalled some of our fondest memories. I also have a checklist with many more old friends I need to contact."

Sowing Seeds

Although some of my life-changers have already been motivated to take a step on their personal gratitude journeys, others have been inspired to at least contemplate the possibility of doing something similar in the future.

Russ Carson said, "I've started to think about seeing my two co-founders more often. They are both less active in the business than I am and live mostly in other parts of the country, so I don't see them nearly as much as I used to. Yet without them, I could not have had the business success and personal satisfaction I've had. I need to think about how I can convey that to them most effectively."

One of my sisters-in-law, Vicki Peterson, is considering adapting an idea that's already meaningful to her. "I'm a great enthusiast of memoir writing, and I've written a few pieces that are connected to important people in my life," she told me. "They weren't written with the idea of being shared until much later in my life. However, I may soon look at them again and edit some or all of them with the idea that this would be a meaningful gift for each of these people. I would also be encouraged to focus on the individuals I *haven't* written about yet."

It would be unreasonable to think that everyone on my victory lap would be inspired to take action. But even those who likely won't be moved to do anything right now may, at the very least, realize that they might feel differently in the future. As Jamie Shapiro, whom I met in a pledge class at the University of Michigan, put it: "In spite of my reticence to be as formal or demonstrative in my appreciation, your friendship and example has left an everlasting positive impression. and I'm grateful for that and feel certain that it will influence me going forward."

Ripples

In the short time since I completed my personal victory lap, I've started hearing about how it's also serving others who weren't part of my journey, and even people whom I've never met. I hope you find the following stories as fascinating as I do.

48 Hours

One driven businessman in his 40s, who heard about my journey from a mutual friend, said that it was life-changing for him. It enabled him to renew his relationship with his grandmother, who'd done everything for him when he was younger except give birth to him.

This man hadn't visited his grandmother in quite a while because he had no patience for spending time with an 88-year-old who, like many elderly people, tended to repeat stories and was hard of hearing. But now he was inspired to call her on a Friday night, and he simply listened to her for an hour. "She so appreciated my time," he said.

The experience made him feel so good that he called her again the next day, talked for another 45 minutes, and then invited her to Sunday brunch. She was so excited that she said she was going to visit the beauty parlor in anticipation of the outing.

When the man and his grandmother saw each other, they cried, realizing how much they valued and missed one another. "There won't be another 48 hours of my life that goes by without my talking to her," he vowed.

Stepping Up

Marla Bingham, a former dancer with the Alvin Ailey American Dance Theater, is my Pilates instructor in San Diego. I told her my story during one of our classes, and it clearly resonated with her: She decided to go to New York and visit some people she hadn't seen in ages. She particularly wanted to pay a visit to Denise, a friend from the dance world, to tell her how she'd impacted her life.

Marla reminded Denise that she'd been the one who'd recommended that she audition for Ailey II, a newly forming dance troupe that was an extension of the original Alvin Ailey company. "I didn't really know the company at the time and just took your advice,

Denise," she said. "I got in! Wow, what a chance! That was the beginning of one of the most important life-changing experiences of my dance career."

Marla acknowledged that Denise's suggestion was likely just a passing comment, but one that came at the right moment, when she was ready for the next step in her career. And it serves to demonstrate that we don't always appreciate the impact we're having on others or where it can take them.

Years later, the two women had another encounter in a workshop, and this time Denise encouraged Marla to choreograph her work in a way that reflected her Native American heritage. "It was you who allowed me to explore and find my identity in an area where I'm now one of the most prominent Native American choreographers, combining traditional tribal dance with ballet and modern," Marla told Denise.

After Marla's New York trip, the two women spoke on the phone. Marla took the opportunity to further let Denise know how much she was respected and valued, not only by her, but by others whom Marla had met over the years.

There was often so much silence on the other end of the phone that Marla thought she'd been disconnected at times. "I didn't realize how special this would be for Denise," she told me. "It started to make me feel so emotional to hear that silence, which meant that she was listening very attentively to my story. It was so great. To express what someone has meant to you is a profound and powerful feeling."

Months later, Marla learned just how much her expression of gratitude had meant to Denise, who'd been suffering from a serious medical issue for some time. Denise said that her old friend's words had been a constant and powerful reminder that she was still capable of doing important work, and it sustained and inspired her during these difficult times.

Marla became emotional telling me this story. She'd clearly experienced the power of expressing profound gratitude, as well as the impact it can have on the recipient. Marla had obviously "stepped up" many times during her distinguished dance career, but I doubt that she ever felt more appreciated and valued than when she "stepped up" for Denise and told her what she had meant to her in her life.

The Send-Off

Another story that touched me deeply came from an acquaintance, Barbara, after I told her about my journey.

Barbara's son, Paul, was in the military, and he was coming home for Christmas before being sent to Afghanistan. Although money was tight, she wanted to do something special for him. "I got an idea when you told me that a lot of times we don't tell people how we feel until it's too late, and then we sit at a funeral wishing we could have said this or that," she told me.

So Barbara had all of her son's loved ones write a letter to him, and on Christmas Eve, Paul sat on a stool and listened as each person read his or her letter out loud to him. Those gathered included the young man's father, who'd flown in from Oregon; his step-father; his grandmothers and a great-grandmother; his sisters; and a couple of close friends; but nothing they expressed could have been perceived as a "final message." Instead, people were humorous and thoughtful in what they had to say, and many noted that they were really looking forward to Paul's homecoming party at the end of his tour of duty.

Barbara said it was a profound experience for everybody to tell this young man what a gift he's been to them over their lifetime, and they were glad Paul received this knowledge before he went away. None of these people would ever have to think, *I wish I would have told him . . .* Instead, as Barbara noted, "Everyone felt good after they'd read their letters, and they thanked me for making this so special."

Paul took the letters with him and prepared to leave with a much fuller heart. But that's not the end of the story.

Barbara told me that right before her son left for Afghanistan, he texted those who'd shared the going-away event with him on Christmas Eve. She proudly showed me the message she'd received, which said, in part, "Thank you for being the best mom any son could ever have."

I asked my friend if he'd written anything like this before and she replied, "No, he's not the expressive type. I think our Christmas letters created the opening."

It was another ripple. I can only think how remarkable and wonderful it would be if all of the men and women who go off to serve our country could do so with the peace of mind that Paul and his family had when he left for Afghanistan.

44 Cents

In closing, I'd like to tell you about "the big man" from Philly. (Since this story involves well-known figures, I'm withholding names to protect their privacy.)

The closest friend of a buddy of mine was a powerful man from Philadelphia who'd been like a big brother to him for more than half a century. This was a "big man" in every respect: he was 6'4" tall and over 240 pounds, as well as a major player in the high echelons of government for many years. There had never been any verbal expressions of affection between the two pals over all those years, in spite of their remarkably close relationship. My friend said that the man from Philly couldn't convey his emotions if you took a chisel and broke his heart open. That's just the way he was.

Now this powerful man was near death, and my friend flew to be with him for five days. In the final moments of their last visit together, the big man rose out of his chair with great difficulty, removed his oxygen mask, put his arm around my friend, and hugged him. My friend told his mentor, "I love you."

And the dying man said, "I know."

Both cried until their shirts were wet from tears. My friend acknowledged that those were two of the most beautiful words he'd ever heard. It was indeed wonderful that they'd been expressed, even at this late hour of their relationship. I asked my buddy what had kept him from hugging his old friend before. He said, "Over 50 years of *not* doing it." It sounds remarkable, but it's probably not that unusual.

After my friend told me about this moving final meeting, I suggested he give some thought to writing a letter to his ailing, treasured confidant, spelling out his feelings before it was too late. He reported to me that he sat down a couple of days later and did just that.

Once he got started, he said that the words started to flow from his pen, and it took him only 15 minutes to write two full pages. My buddy was able to say things that he could never have expressed in person.

After receiving this letter, the man from Philly called my friend and, through his tears, articulated his total appreciation and love. My buddy cried as well. Although this call only lasted about five minutes, he told me that he felt a real sense of closure. "I have nothing more I need to say," my friend explained. "I didn't feel that way after spending five *days* with him."

You might think that a cross-country visit would

have been enough to speak volumes in and of itself. But that's not true; important things were still left unsaid between these two old friends. *Expressing one's gratitude is hard to accomplish without actually using words.*

Older men—especially, I suspect, when they've been in the military—find this type of expression challenging. But this is a profound example of how two old warriors overcame their natural reticence and how much it ultimately meant to them.

And what did this amazing sense of closure and peace of mind cost my friend? Fifteen minutes; two pieces of stationery; one envelope; and a 44-cent stamp.

℘ ℘ ℘

If these highly private, stoic types can express their gratitude, then I believe that any one of you can. What I am most hopeful for, however, is that you're now inspired to find an uncommon way to express your gratitude to *someone* who has made a real difference in your life.

℘ ℘ ℘ ℘ ℘

AFTERWORD

*"A man's growth is seen
in the successive choirs
of his friends."*

— RALPH WALDO EMERSON

I am by nature a private person, except among those with whom I've built long and dear relationships. Sharing my intimate relationships with a wider audience has definitely taken me out of my comfort zone. Yet despite that, I felt that the lessons to be learned from this experience were too important not to be conveyed.

It's very fulfilling to spread the word of extraordinary gratitude. I'm glad that you've taken the time to read this book and to consider taking gratitude's "road less traveled" yourself. I'd be very surprised if, after taking action, you didn't find the experience very rewarding and look forward to doing it more.

From the outset, writing this book has been all about capturing the opportunity to express heartfelt appreciation before it's too late. I didn't share my journey because I feel you should try to replicate it; rather, I wanted to give you the inspiration to create your own path that makes sense for you and the people you want to honor. I strongly encourage you to express gratitude to at least one person and then decide for yourself if you wish to do more.

I certainly plan to do more. When I started out, I thought that my journey would have a beginning and an end. Then again, learning never has a beginning and an end for me—it's a lifelong endeavor. I live to learn; and I learn in order to teach, coach, support, and show my affection.

I've listened to each of the audio recordings I made with my life-changers more than once. Every time I've done so, it has brought back memories of those milestone conversations and left me with a deeper appreciation of my treasured relationships and of myself. It's a bit like watching a classic movie: every time you see it, you notice another nuance or receive another message. These CDs are now my most cherished collection of lifetime memories that, like works of art, I'll enjoy for many years to come.

And yes, my conversations will continue as well. I've become acutely aware that expressing profound gratitude has become a way of life for me.

Ideal Outcomes

I'm hopeful that this book will create a shift in gratitude consciousness and expression. I've always framed my future in terms of ideal outcomes, so one ideal outcome for me would be if this ultimately became a transformational action plan in the tradition of the "pay it forward" movement. Each of you would express uncommon gratitude to people in your own life, and they in turn would express their appreciation to others. It would be a real game-changer, with the potential to make all of us far more fulfilled and gratified. My hope is that this book will make *everyone's* game better.

As I was drawing to the end of writing *This Is the Moment!* I told a friend about it. I loved that he was so anxious to read the book, but I was especially encouraged when he immediately mentioned how he could *use* it. He shared with me that over the years, he'd often send books that he considered important to his friends, business colleagues, clients, and family members.

"Walter, your book would be a perfect way to wrap up my expression of gratitude to people," he told me. "It would be far more effective than some other book and a card. I can inscribe each copy with my own message of gratitude, telling the person what he or she has meant to me." And then, he said, with a glitter in his eyes, "Yes, this *is* the moment!"

Whether this particular idea resonates with you or not, I want to encourage you to leave everything on the field of gratitude.

℘ ℘ ℘

After I finished writing this book, I was at a social function and happened to be discussing the message of *This Is the Moment!* with a woman I'd just met. About a week later, I received an e-mail from her, which was so touching that I wanted to share the contents with you. Here's what she wrote me:

> *I told you I had a third/fourth-grade teacher whom I had fond remembrances of all these years. I said I had always wanted to write her a letter but never did. Well, I came home after talking to you and wrote that letter. I have now spent all week tracking down former classmates to find Miss Carson's address. In the process, many of them shared fond stories with me of our favorite teacher.*
>
> *The best story was when we left fourth grade, knowing that she would not be our teacher the next year, and we each wrote her a letter. Fast-forward to the summer of 2008. Miss Carson was in the hospital to have surgery, and a former student went to visit her. At one point, Miss Carson said, "Please bring me that briefcase over there." Inside was a manila folder, and it had all of the letters we had written to her upon leaving*

the fourth grade. She cherished those letters so much that she had kept them all these years. She even called them her "love notes."

Miss Carson is probably in her mid-80s now; has recovered; and is driving around Muncie, Indiana, in a sporty little car. She never had children and only taught grade school for the two years we had her. Yet she considers us all her children.

I am sure that she will be thrilled to hear from me. I updated her on what I have done since leaving high school, etc. I feel both relieved and joyful to have written that letter. And I have a very nostalgic part of me that harkens back to third and fourth grade because of that wonderful, loving teacher. Teachers are not well paid, and the least we can do is pay them in thank-yous.

Thanks for nudging me forward.

This book went to press before I found out what Miss Carson's response was to this heartfelt expression of gratitude from her former student. I hope my acquaintance will drop me a line and let me know how everything turned out.

I'd also love to hear from *you* about your own experiences and what they meant to you and the person you were acknowledging. Please share your story with me on my Website: **thisisthemoment.org**.

@ @ @

Another ideal outcome for me would be to have a conversation of gratitude many years from now with my grandchildren, Claire and Wilson, who are now six and seven years old. (In the meantime, I know that they're being loved, nourished, and appreciated by their remarkable parents, Ann and Jason.)

When it comes time to have this conversation, wouldn't it be wonderful if expressing deep gratitude wasn't so out of the ordinary by then? I think that if increased awareness—initiated with this book and paid forward by you—can create a new customary behavior, then hopefully during their lifetime, my grandchildren (and yours) will routinely come to pay tribute to their parents and others in their lives. Expressing profound gratitude won't be uncommon; it will just be "the way it's done." It will be as natural as when we now say "Thank you" or "I love you." And if that's the case, it would be a legacy I'd be very proud of.

For you and for those whom you love and honor, I am hopeful that *This Is the Moment!*

Bibliography

These are a few of the books that have influenced me in my life, and have inspired some of the ideas I've presented in this book:

Albom, Mitch. *Tuesdays with Morrie.* Doubleday, 1997.

Blanchard, Ken. *Leading at a Higher Level.* FT Press, 2006.

Buchwald, Art. *Too Soon to Say Goodbye.* Random House, 2006.

Chapman, Gary. *The Five Love Languages.* Northfield Publishing, 1995 (reprinted 2010).

Crowley, Chris; and Lodge, Henry, M.D. *Younger Next Year.* Workman Publishing, 2007.

Emmons, Robert, Ph.D. *Thanks!* Mariner Books, 2008.

Kielburger, Craig; and Kielburger, Marc. *Me to We.* Fireside, 2006.

Lyubomirsky, Sonja. *The How of Happiness.* Penguin Press, 2007.

Nerburn, Kent. *Letters to My Son.* New World Library, 1994 (revised 1999).

O'Kelly, Eugene. *Chasing Daylight*. McGraw Hill, 2007.

O'Toole, James. *Creating the Good Life*. Rodale Books, 2005.

Pausch, Randy. *The Last Lecture*. Hyperion, 2008.

Qubein, Nido. *Stairway to Success*. Wiley, 1997.

Russert, Tim. *Wisdom of Our Fathers*. Random House, 2006.

Seligman, Martin, Ph.D. *Authentic Happiness*. Free Press, 2004.

Somers, Suzanne. *Breakthrough*. Three Rivers Press, 2009.

Tolle, Eckhart. *The Power of Now*. New World Library, 1999.

Waitley, Dennis. *Seeds of Greatness*. Pocket Books, 1988.

℘ ℘ ℘ ℘ ℘

ACKNOWLEDGMENTS

Although *This Is the Moment!* focuses on one very special year of my life, it is the product of a lifetime of experiences and relationships. To all of you who have touched my life along the way, please understand that whether or not you were mentioned in the pages of this book, you have left a mark on my heart that will be everlasting.

To the many talented, caring, and dedicated fellow members of the Harrison Conference Center team, my deepest gratitude to you for making the main event of my business life so fulfilling and rewarding. You made me very proud. And for those I have known in professional organizations over the years, including the Young Presidents' Organization, World Presidents' Organization, Chief Executives Organization, and L3 Organization (Leadership, Legacy and Life), I am very grateful for the relationships and personal development that have been part of these experiences. They have indeed enriched my life.

To my family and my family of friends, there is no life without you. Your inspiration, your love, your support, and your presence in my life has been my greatest blessing. And to my wife, Lola, your imprint

and impact is ever present, and this book is no exception. Without your gift of time, I never would have
been able to take my yearlong gratitude journey. And
without your wide circle of friends and relationships, I
wouldn't have had that serendipitous meeting with Jill
Kramer, the editorial director of Hay House.

My journey of gratitude has heightened my sense
of awareness that I'm indeed not self-made. So it is
with the publication of *This Is the Moment!* There is no
way this book would be in your hands today without
the talent, support, and enthusiasm of several people. I
will never forget my initial meeting at Hay House with
Jill Kramer and Reid Tracy, the company's CEO and
president, and how the message of this book resonated
with them both. Their enthusiastic support has never
wavered throughout the publication process.

During that initial meeting, I also mentioned that,
although I had a lot of experience with the spoken
word over the years and had written on occasion, I'd
never authored a book before. I was up front and said
that I'd need help. Jill provided me with several names,
which led me to Angela Hynes.

Angela was the perfect collaborator for me. She
fully grasped that the most important outcome for me
was that the book successfully convey the power of
extraordinary gratitude, and that my life story and the
stories of those on my journey be highlighted only as
a composer would develop melodies to create memorable music.

My preparatory notes of my conversations of gratitude, the hours and hours of recordings with people on my journey, and other material I'd written along the way had been organized by my assistant, Christy Barwick, but it was a major task to convert this material into a book. Angela and I spent hours and even days together to try to get it just right. Quite simply, I could not have done this book without her. I am deeply grateful to her for her writing talent, her commitment to this project, her remarkable organizational skills, her patience with the pursuit of perfection, and her capacity to capture both my words and my message.

I would be remiss if I failed to mention that I formed a "library cabinet"—my personal sounding board comprised of Jeff Stiefler, Tommy Schulhof, and Stephen Miron—who provided me with suggestions and feedback from the initial structure of the book to its final copy. You've read about these gentlemen in *This Is the Moment!* However, I should also mention that it was Jeff who recommended that I record these conversations of gratitude, which was a brilliant idea.

At Hay House, I was so fortunate to have the talents and experience of senior editor, Shannon Littrell. Her input and counsel was only equaled by her enthusiasm for the book. Shannon was an absolute pleasure to work with, and I couldn't have found a more supportive editor.

After the contents of the book were set, I had the good fortune to be able to work on the jacket cover design with Julie Davison, a senior designer at Hay House. Julie was able to capture the feelings and look that I was hoping for in the cover and could not have been more collegial to work with.

And last but not least, I'd like to express the following to each and every person on my journey: not only am I grateful for your contribution to my life, but I also greatly appreciate your willingness to let me use your names and excerpt whatever I wanted from our intimate conversations, in order to be as helpful to the reader as possible. My decision to use more or less of any individual conversation was only a reflection of what I thought would serve the purposes of the book, and I am so grateful to all of you for your understanding and unbridled support.

This Is the Moment! has been written to elevate our consciousness and expression of gratitude. In the process, I hope that I have adequately recognized those on my yearlong journey; as well as the multitude of others who have touched my heart, my mind, and my soul on my *life's* journey.

About the Author

Walter Green was Chairman of the Board and CEO of Harrison Conference Services for 25 years, during which time it grew into the leading conference center management company in the U.S. He has lectured at the Wharton Graduate School of Business and Hofstra and Long Island universities, as well as being featured as an expert on the topic of effective meetings in numerous national publications. Associated for years with the Young Presidents' Organization and the World Presidents' Organization, he's presently a member of the Chief Executives Organization and the L3 Organization (Leadership, Legacy, Life). Since selling his company, he mentors young adults and is actively involved with several nonprofit organizations. He lives with his wife, Lola, in San Diego, California.

Please visit: **thisisthemoment.org**.

NOTES

NOTES

NOTES

NOTES

NOTES

NOTES

NOTES

NOTES